# MR SPEAKER, SIR

*Selwyn Lloyd*

JONATHAN CAPE
THIRTY BEDFORD SQUARE LONDON

FIRST PUBLISHED 1976

© 1976 BY LORD SELWYN-LLOYD

JONATHAN CAPE LTD
30 BEDFORD SQUARE, LONDON WCI


British Library Cataloguing in Publication Data
Lloyd, Selwyn
Mr Speaker, sir.
Index
ISBN 0–224–01318–1
1. Title
328.41'07'62 JN 678
Great Britain – Parliament – House of Commons –
Speaker – History


PRINTED IN GREAT BRITAIN
BY EBENEZER BAYLIS & SON, LIMITED
THE TRINITY PRESS, WORCESTER, AND LONDON

# MR SPEAKER,
## SIR

*For Joanna*

# Contents

# Illustrations

# Acknowledgments

I would like to thank The Bodley Head for permission to quote from Arthur Irwin Dasent, *The Speakers of the House of Commons* (1911); Cassell and Co. Ltd for permission to quote from Sir Winston Churchill, *History of the English-Speaking Peoples*, vol. II (1956); Cassell and Co. Ltd and the author for permission to quote from Philip Laundy, *The Office of Speaker* (1964); Methuen and Co. Ltd for permission to quote from Michael MacDonagh, *The Speaker of the House* (1914); and the Trustees of the Erskine May Trust for permission to quote from Erskine May, *Treatise on the Laws, Privileges, Proceedings and Usages of Parliament*, 18th edn (1971).

# Introduction

With some hesitation, I have decided to write this account of my time as Speaker.

My predecessors appear to have been reticent about publishing accounts of their periods of office.

Speaker Denison (1857–72) kept a journal. It was found many years later, without any instructions as to what was to be done with it. A few copies were printed for private circulation, one of which reached the House of Commons Library. I have quoted from it more than once.

Speaker Brand (1872–84) left papers, diaries, and letters covering *inter alia* his time as Speaker. So far as I know, they were never published, but they have been listed by the House of Lords Record Office, and are available to be read. When I went through his diaries about what was happening in the House of Commons a hundred years ago, they were so well written that I felt I was re-living almost every moment of his time. The procedures were different, but otherwise very little seems to have changed in the atmosphere of the House, and the problems confronting the Speaker in his relations with individual Members. Nor were his difficulties limited to the handling of the Irish Nationalists.

Speaker Lowther (1905–21) published two volumes of memoirs in 1925, giving a detailed account of his political life before and while he was Speaker. As he was undoubtedly high on the list of outstanding Speakers, they have been of great assistance to me in writing this book.

Speaker King wrote a delightful little book, with imaginative and excellent illustrations, published in 1973 and called *The Speaker and Parliament*. It was intended for use in schools, to explain what happens in Parliament and the role of the Speaker.

In this book I have attempted something which I do not think has been attempted before: that is a detailed account of the Speaker's duties and responsibilities, and the way in which an individual Speaker tried to discharge them. It will not be an embarrassment to my successors, because each Speaker must be a law unto himself within the bounds laid down by the Standing Orders and the customs of the House. Each Speaker must set his own style.

This book is not a chronological record or a diary. There is quite a long chapter dealing with the origins and development of the Speakership. I want to make it clear that I have written it without the help of research assistants, but I have drawn freely upon books already published. I list them gratefully: the masterly work of my friend Philip Laundy, *The Office of Speaker* (1964); the interesting book *The Speakers of the House of Commons* (1911) by Arthur Irwin Dasent, then Clerk in the Duchy of Lancaster office, afterwards for a short time Clerk of the Journals, House of Commons, and then Clerk of the Parliaments in Northern Ireland 1924–9; a rather more racy account, *The Speaker of the House* (1914) by Michael MacDonagh, written with twenty-four years experience behind him of what he describes as 'The Reporters' Gallery'; a book by an old friend from the Press Gallery, Graham Cawthorne, written twenty-five years ago, which he also called *Mr Speaker, Sir*; and finally Erskine May's *Treatise on the Laws, Privileges, Proceedings and Usages of Parliament*. I have had to be content with the 18th edition (1971), but I understand a 19th edition will be in print before this book. It contains the distilled knowledge and wisdom of its editors, and remains the fount of knowledge about the Standing Orders, conventions and practices of the House. I suppose that I used to consult it at least once daily.

But my real purpose in writing this book has been to try to give an impression of the Speaker's day-to-day life while the House is sitting. I have tried to describe the scope of his activities and responsibilities, the way in which I myself carried them out, the strains and stresses under which any Speaker works, his social and representative functions, and the general background to an office of which I believe little is known, in spite of its antiquity and prestige. Some think that to call a man Speaker who does not make speeches is a touch of parliamentary humour. This is one of several misconceptions about the House of Commons which I hope to dispel or at least explain.

Every Speaker knows that his behaviour is under close scrutiny and subject to constant criticism. His hope is that the criticisms will come in equal measure from both sides of the House. If he is too authoritative, he is likely to be called arrogant. If he lets the House discipline itself, or fails to do so himself, he is called weak. He can never do exactly right, or satisfy completely the other 634 Members.

I have said that each Speaker must set his own style. When Speaker Denison died, his obituary in *The Times* contained this passage: 'The guiding touch of the presiding hand is not most truly felt in calls to order, or sonorous decisions, but in the silent influence of personal character, and in quiet suggestions of temperate advice, by smoothing away difficulties, rather than in repressing discord.' To say that during my time I tried to follow those guide lines may indeed sound presumptuous. I do however believe that they are the guide lines for a modern Speaker. That they were written on 18th March 1873 goes to illustrate yet again the continuity of the office of Speaker.

On one aspect of my time as Speaker, I can be quite dogmatic. I owe a large debt of gratitude to many people: the two Clerks of the House during my time, Sir Barnett Cocks and Sir David Lidderdale; their Clerks Assistant, and all the others in the Clerk's Department; my Counsel, Sir Robert Speed; the Serjeant at Arms and his staff; those concerned with the Library, *Hansard* and the delivery of the vote; the refreshment department; the police; the custodians; and that host of unseen men and women, the maintenance men, the cleaners, the furniture movers, all of whom help to make the Palace of Westminster function efficiently in its various capacities.

More closely concerned with my daily activities were my secretary, Brigadier Short, and the Trainbearers for four and a half years, Mr Green and Mr Canter, joined in the last few months by Mr Lord. All who worked in my private office were helpful and loyal to a degree for which gratitude cannot be expressed in words.

Next I mention my Deputies in the order in which they were appointed to help the Speaker — Rt Hon. Sir Robert Grant-Ferris, Deputy Speaker, now Lord Harvington; Miss Harvie Anderson, Deputy Chairman of Ways and Means, now a Privy Councillor; Lance Mallalieu, Second Deputy Chairman of Ways and Means, now Sir Lance Mallalieu; Rt Hon. Oscar Murton, now Deputy Speaker; Rt Hon. George Thomas, my successor as Speaker; and Sir Myer Galpern, now First Deputy Chairman of Ways and Means. I owed them much for their loyal co-operation, consideration and help. I do not think that there was ever a cross word between us.

I must also thank those who kindly read through my drafts, and made many helpful suggestions. I will not name them lest blame should be imputed to them for shortcomings which are mine alone.

Finally, my thanks are due to my personal staff, the indefatigable Miss Susan Carter, who typed the drafts when she could find time amid all the constituency and other letters, and Christopher Spence, my personal assistant, whose comments and encouragement were a great help. But for them, I do not think that this book would have been written.

1976

# *I*

# My Election

If anyone had prophesied to me on 12th January 1970 that one year later I should be elected Speaker of the House of Commons, I should have been very surprised, to put it mildly.

It came about in this way. Early in 1970 Vere Harvey, the Chairman of the Conservative 1922 Committee, raised the subject with me. The Chairman of this Committee has always exercised considerable influence within the Party and with its leaders, and an approach from him had to be taken seriously.

Harvey said to me that Horace King had been Speaker for four and a half years and would not want to continue for long in the next Parliament. If the Conservatives won the next election, they would have the choice of Speaker when King retired. There was substance in this. Although the Speaker should be the choice of the whole House, a new Speaker would probably come from the Party with a majority. He asked me whether I would like to be Speaker. I replied that the idea had never entered my head, but if the Party did win the election I would think it over. There were plenty of arguments for and against. However, I thought that the first thing was to see who won the election.

In June 1970 the Conservatives were victorious, and when the House assembled Harvey returned to the subject. He asked me to think seriously about it. He had reason to believe that King would retire on his seventieth birthday in May 1971.

I began to consider the pros and cons without any sense of urgency. Then in September or early October, King said that he wished to retire in January 1971, immediately after a visit which he was planning to pay to India for a Commonwealth Speakers' Conference. Willie Whitelaw, who was Leader of the House and knew about my talk with Harvey, asked me for a definite answer. Did I want to be Speaker? If I did, he was certain that I would be elected.

Accepting the Speakership meant severing my connection with the Conservative Party, in particular its fortunes in the north west and all the congenial friendships which I had formed there. It is the convention that a Speaker must not only be impartial and separated from any Party political arguments during his Speakership, but he must also remain detached when his period of office is over, and if he goes to the House of Lords sit upon the cross benches. Above all this would mean the end of the cameraderie of the House of Commons, and the friendly exchanges of Smoking Room, Annie's Bar, the tea-room, the lobby and the corridors. At the age of sixty-six I would be entering on a mode of life which, while the House was sitting, would tie me to the Palace of Westminster with little chance of exercise or outside activities other than official duties. It would be strenuous, tiring and involve constant strain.

It would also mean the sacrifice of my business interests. At that time I was a director of the Sun Alliance Assurance Company and Chairman of its Overseas Committee. I was also a director of the Rank Organization, the English and Caledonian Investment Co., the I.D.C. Group, and of a private company in Liverpool. Provided I kept my health, I could probably continue with all these for another ten years or so, except with the Sun Alliance where there was a strict retiring age.

On the other side of the balance, the Speakership is a great office with seven hundred years of tradition behind it.

Mr Speaker comes sixth in the order of precedence after members of the Royal Family. (The order is Archbishop of Canterbury, Lord Chancellor, Archbishop of York, Prime Minister, Lord President of the Council, Mr Speaker and the Lord Privy Seal.) And it would be a challenge. I loved the House of Commons. Obviously there were troubles facing it comparable to those of 1909–13, or of the nineteenth century, when the Irish members first emerged as an obstructive element in the House. With my experience, perhaps I could serve the House in this last phase of my career there.

Although one or two of my friends made cautionary noises, most of those whom I consulted were very much in favour of it. Bob Mellish, the Labour Chief Whip, said that 'his boys' were all for me. In fact, unless they had a written assurance from me that I had been offered it and turned it down, they would not support any other Tory.

Accordingly, I told Whitelaw that my answer was a definite 'yes'. Then the trouble began. There were two things which I did not know. First, although the two Chief Whips had consulted some people, they had not done a comprehensive exercise with their back-benchers. The Liberals had not been consulted at all. Secondly, I did not know that I was likely to be faced with the possibility of a disagreeable contest.

No sooner had I decided to accept and made it known, than I found that John Boyd-Carpenter, a friend and colleague since 1945, was also a candidate; and, after some heart-searching, had decided that he would welcome the position. Had I known that earlier, I might have decided differently. But having made up my mind to accept, and in view of Mellish's statement, I felt that I must persist.

In due course the Cabinet took up the position that it would support whichever of the two of us had most support in the Labour Shadow Cabinet. The Shadow Cabinet voted in my favour, by a substantial majority I was told, and the Cabinet decided to support me.

The Press got to know, or were told, and it was reported in the newspapers as fact that I was to be the new Speaker.

Then the storm broke. Back-benchers on both sides felt that they had not been properly consulted; and that a decision by the two front benches in a matter essentially for the whole House was being thrust down their throats. They were determined to assert their rights.

The tide began to run against me. There was some doubt about how decisive the Shadow Cabinet's view had been. It was put to me that I should withdraw. In the event it was Boyd-Carpenter who magnanimously stood down; but even after that the name of a fresh opponent was put forward in the Press almost daily.

The election took place on 12th January 1971, the first sitting day after the Christmas recess. It was a dramatic and traumatic day.

I walked down to the House from my flat in St James's Court. I had agreed to be photographed outside St Stephen's Entrance at noon. I went to my room, came down for perhaps my last visit to the Smoking Room as a Member, and returned to my flat for lunch. About 2.20 p.m. I went back to the House and into the Chamber.

The House was packed, as also were all the Strangers' Galleries. I sat in my usual seat at the end of the third row below the gangway instead of the end of the third row above the gangway where the Speaker-Elect has usually sat in my time. It was not always so. Speaker Denison states in his journal that he took his seat 'about the middle of the bench below the gangway on the Ministerial side of the House, on the floor'. I wore a blue suit instead of the traditional morning coat. I did not want anyone to think that I was taking the result for granted.

I had been assured that all would go well, but no one had any idea of the number who would vote against me. There was obvious tension in the air. I wondered whether it would be a humiliating vote.

The Prime Minister was away so Reginald Maudling

acted for him. The Clerk of the House from the lower chair stood up and pointed to Maudling, who then said, 'Sir Barnett Cocks, I have to acquaint the House that Her Majesty, having been informed of the resignation of the Right Honourable Horace King, lately Speaker of this House gives leave to the House to proceed forthwith to the choice of a new Speaker.'

Dame Irene Ward, who first entered the House in 1931 and was renowned for her robust independence, had agreed to propose me, and Charles Pannell, a former Labour Minister and a Privy Councillor, had agreed to second me. He had always taken a great interest in procedure and the running of the House of Commons.

They did so with generous speeches. Charles Taylor made a non-controversial intervention. Then John Pardoe, Liberal Member for North Cornwall, Robin Maxwell-Hyslop, Conservative Member for Tiverton, and Willie Hamilton, Labour Member for West Fife, all spoke against the proposition.

The speeches of these three Members were moderate in tone, courteous towards me personally, and listened to quietly on the whole by a crowded House.

I will try to set out their arguments in some detail.

Pardoe said that he was dissatisfied with the procedure. In the war to control the executive, the right of the House of Commons to elect its Speaker was one of our most significant victories. The Speaker should be the servant of the House and not of the executive. Very few Members believed that they had been consulted in any meaningful sense of the word. So far as he knew, the Parliamentary Labour Party had not been consulted, nor the 1922 Committee, nor even the Executive Committee of the 1922 Committee. The House as a whole should have chosen between me and Boyd-Carpenter.

Then he developed a rather different argument. He said that the Speaker should not be a former senior Minister. 'Can a man imbued with the rights of Government ever throw off that mode of thinking entirely?' He said that he did not feel too unhappy on that account so far as I was concerned. But it was wrong to have an ex-Minister because he could not fail to be a figure of controversy.

Maxwell-Hyslop followed and stated that he agreed with almost everything that Pardoe had said. The House of Commons had had no opportunity to participate in the choice. Members had not been consulted. He emphasized the great influence which a Speaker can have on the business of the House, allowing debates under Standing Order No. 9, selecting amendments on Report Stages, and so on. He also developed a procedural point, to which he attached much importance, as to whether there could be a division without an alternative candidate. To be certain of a division, he nominated Geoffrey de Freitas, to the consternation of de Freitas himself.

Hamilton seconded the nomination of de Freitas. He said that there was nothing personal against me in his approach. I quote what he said because he is known to have strong views on many matters, and to speak his mind without fear or favour.

It is not trite to say that no Member of the House who has had experience of the right hon. and learned gentleman, either as a Minister or as a back-bencher, but particularly as a Minister in his last office, would deny that he has served the House and the country very well indeed. Every hon. Member who has spoken in this debate has spoken not out of enmity or disfavour of the right hon. and learned gentleman, but because of the procedures which have brought us to this position. The right hon. and learned gentleman was one of the best Leaders of the House under whom I have had the privilege to serve and in view of that experience, I am completely satisfied that under his Speakership, the rights of the back-bench Members will be completely safeguarded.

But he objected to the lack of consultation, and felt that there should have been an emergency party meeting so that they could have gone through the process of consultation.

He asked that the Committee of Procedure should consider a more democratic way of going through the process of electing a Speaker.

He then referred to the custom of not electing a Member who has held ministerial office. He put the arguments for this: a back-bencher was best able to understand the wishes and frustrations of fellow back-benchers; he was less likely to yield to the blandishments of Ministers. Hamilton objected to the election of a Member who had held highly controversial office. He referred to Suez in 1956 when I was Foreign Secretary and to the remuneration of nurses in 1961 when I was Chancellor. When he had finished, I said my piece. It was very brief. De Freitas spoke next and said that he would vote for me.

A division followed. The tellers for the ayes were Dame Irene Ward and Pannell, and those for the noes Maxwell-Hyslop and Hamilton. The figures were 294 for the ayes and 55 against. The Cabinet and Shadow Cabinet had manfully stuck to their choice, although there were one or two surprising names among the 55.

I believe that the opponents had good grounds for their point about consultation — every Member ought to be consulted in some way. I also think that there was substance in Maxwell-Hyslop's procedural point. This was subsequently put right in Standing Order No. 103A, which was passed in 1972.

I disagree with the argument that an ex-Minister should not become Speaker, but I do not think that a Minister should go direct from office to the Speaker's Chair. That happened with Hylton-Foster. Although it could be said that the office of Solicitor-General, which he held, is detached from acute party controversy, I do not think it a good precedent. W. S. Morrison had been a member of Churchill's Consultative Committee, i.e., his Shadow

Cabinet. During that time he had not taken a very prominent part in controversial debates, but he had sat on the front bench. I do not think that it is a good precedent for an ex-Minister or indeed anyone to go from the Opposition front bench to the Chair.

In my own case, I had left the Opposition front bench in April 1966, more than four and a half years before. I had taken little or no part in controversial debates after that. In my view, I had had a sufficient period of quarantine.

On this point, I was very pleased to hear what Harold Wilson had to say in March 1974, when he was congratulating me on my re-election. 'I have been a strong opponent of the practice which developed in the early 1950s of electing ex-Ministers to the Speakership. It is a tribute to you, Mr Speaker-Elect, in your tenure of this demanding office, that you have largely converted me from that 20-year opinion.'

In October 1974, when congratulating me again upon my election as Speaker, he returned to this theme, and said,

> As you will know, Mr Speaker-Elect, I was in past years something of an opponent of the practice of electing the Speaker from the ranks of those who formerly held ministerial office. That had been my view, which I expressed on many occasions, for almost 20 years. Your own distinguished service in many of the highest offices in the land would not perhaps originally have commended itself to me as a qualification for the Speakership, though when your name was first proposed by the right hon. Gentleman the Leader of the Opposition I felt that on personal grounds I would wish to support it strongly. On successive occasions when the choice of this House fell upon you I have been happy to move further from my original view. I have done so not on personal grounds but on your record in the Chair.

He spoke again to the same effect in February 1976 when I retired from the Speakership. I believe that it is of benefit to the Speaker to have been a Minister. He knows how Departments work, and, so far from yielding to the blandishments of Ministers, he is better able to withstand them. But there should be this period of quarantine or detachment from the front bench, whether Government or Opposition.

After the vote I was conducted to the Chair. The Speaker-Elect is supposed to show reluctance and be dragged towards the Chair by his proposer and seconder. On this occasion I did not think it fair to Irene Ward and Pannell to subject them to this physical test. I went willingly.

Standing on the upper step to the Chair, I thanked the House for the honour which had been paid me, and told those who had spoken and voted against me that I would have no hard feelings at all with regard to that matter in the future.

I then took the Chair, and the Serjeant at Arms, Rear-Admiral Gordon Lennox, placed the Mace upon the Table.

Maudling, Wilson, Jeremy Thorpe and Robin Turton, the Father of the House, congratulated me. By then it was 4.10 p.m. and at the end of the speeches Maudling said, 'I have to signify that it is Her Majesty's pleasure that this House should present their Speaker on this day at 5.15 p.m. in the House of Peers, for Her Majesty's Royal approbation.'

I suspended the sitting and went off to Speaker's House, for the first time in my own right, to put on the appropriate clothes. They are the legal court dress of a Queen's Counsel, with knee breeches instead of trousers, long black stockings and buckled shoes. Normally the Speaker wears on top of them a black gown, and on his head a full-bottomed wig. For this occasion only, he wears no gown and only a bobtailed wig. The origin of this custom is obscure. One story is that Speaker Denison objected to walking through cold and draughty corridors with his head uncovered. As the Clerks wore bobtailed wigs, he decided that he would do the same. I have no idea whether this is authentic.

The robes are one of the problems of a newly elected

Speaker. Because there can be no certainty beforehand that he will be elected, he cannot order his own in advance. Indeed, if it were known that he had done so, there would be trouble. So he has to rely upon the goodwill of his predecessor and trust that the fit will be reasonable. King, as I expected, was kindness itself. His coat fitted me fairly well but the breeches were much too small; I had to conceal the sartorial gap with a black cummerbund. I could just manage with his buckled shoes. Messrs Ede and Ravenscroft later did an excellent rushed job in making new robes, but for the first few days ill-fitting garments did not add to my self-confidence.

It was just the same with the full-bottomed wig. King's did not fit me very well, but Hartley Shawcross, with characteristic thoughtfulness, remembered that it was twenty years since I had practised at the Bar. On the morning of 12th January, he sent his own wig round to the House of Commons, with a note saying that he had no doubt that I had sold mine and I might like to have his for as long as I was Speaker. He was right—I had sold mine. The wig was sent round to my private secretary, Miss Susan Carter, in the morning, well before my election. She had to take delivery of this strange parcel in the room she shared with other secretaries and try to conceal its contents until after the vote.

At 5.15 p.m. I returned to the Chamber, glad that the ordeal of election was over, but not very comfortable in my robes. Black Rod, or to give him his full title the Gentleman Usher of the Black Rod, Sir Frank Twiss, came from the Lords to summon me thither. In accordance with custom and to show the Commons' independence of the Lords, the door was shut in his face. He had to knock and ask permission to enter the Commons. He summoned us to the Lords.

I went along with him on my right and the Serjeant at Arms on my left, carrying the Mace on his arm to show that I was not yet approved as Speaker. We were followed by a

number of Members. The Commissioners sitting in front of
the throne with Lord Hailsham, the Lord Chancellor, were
Earl Jellicoe, the Leader of the House, the Earl of Listowel,
Lord Rea and Lord Shackleton, all in their robes. We
bowed three times, and after each bow they raised their
hats. I said,

My Lords, I have to inform your Lordships that Her
Majesty's faithful Commons, in obedience to the Royal
Command, and in the exercise of their undoubted
rights and privileges, have proceeded to the election of a
Speaker and that their choice has fallen on me. I therefore present myself for Her Majesty's gracious approbation.

The Commission having been read, the Lord Chancellor
said,

Mr Selwyn Lloyd, we have it in command from Her
Majesty to declare Her Majesty's entire confidence in
your talents, diligence and sufficiency to fulfil the important duties of the high Office of Speaker of the
House of Commons to which you have been chosen by
that House; and in obedience to the Commission which
has been read, and by virtue of the authority therein
contained, we do declare Her Majesty's Royal allowance and confirmation upon you, Sir, as Speaker of the
House of Commons.

I replied,

My Lords, I submit myself with all humility to Her
Majesty's Royal will and pleasure, and if, in the discharge of my duties and in the maintenance of the
rights and privileges of the Commons House of Parliament, I should inadvertently fall into error, I pray that
the blame may be imputed to me alone and not to Her
Majesty's faithful Commons.

We then retired. On reaching the Commons and after bowing to the Chair, I walked straight through to the small room at the back of it, and put on my gown and full-bottomed wig. Then, clad for the first time in my proper dress, I took the Chair. I reported Her Majesty's approbation of my choice and said, 'My first duty in the House is to repeat my respectful acknowledgment of the honour it has done me, and the confidence it has reposed in me, and to renew my assurances of my entire devotion to the service of the House.'

I then put the Question 'That this House do now adjourn', and left the Chamber at 5.33 p.m.

I was certainly not the first Speaker whose election was attended by controversy and I had no hard feelings.

Dasent published his book in 1911. He had had long experience of the House. In fact, in his introduction, he described how as a child he had been held up by his nurse at a window to see Palmerston's coffin carried into Westminster Abbey. Nevertheless, when I read his account of Speaker Denison's progress to the Chair in 1857, I could not help feeling a little envious. Dasent wrote that, to his knowledge, Palmerston consulted Delane, the editor of *The Times*, about the credentials of the various candidates for the Speakership when Speaker Shaw-Lefevre retired in 1857. Delane listed the essential qualifications as follows,

(1) imperturbable good temper, tact, patience and urbanity;

(2) a previous legal training, if possible;

(3) absence of bitter partisanship in his previous career;

(4) the possession of innate gentlemanly feelings which involuntarily command respect and deference;

(5) personal dignity in voice and manner.

Dasent added that Delane might have included the importance of a sense of humour.

Upon this recipe for perfection, Palmerston acted. Denison, somewhat to his surprise, received a letter from Palmerston in admirably succinct terms.

*7 April 1857*                                     *94 Piccadilly*

My dear Denison,
    We wish to propose you for the Speakership of the House of Commons. Will you agree?
                              Yours sincerely,
                              PALMERSTON

After making some inquiries, Denison agreed. The entry in his journal reads, 'I was chosen Speaker on 30th April, 1857, unanimously and therefore without a vote, chosen not elected.'

After my rather more controversial experience in January 1971, I soon began to get my second wind, with the time and inclination to study the development of the Speakership.

## II

# My Predecessors

This chapter, about those who held the Speakership before me, is not the result of deep research. I have relied upon the books referred to in the Introduction, and particularly upon those written by Laundy, Dasent and MacDonagh. I would not discourage any reader who has got so far from skipping it. I myself, however, have been extremely interested to read how the role of the Speaker has changed and his authority grown through the centuries. I do not believe it possible to understand how the House functions today, without some appreciation of the way it has developed its Standing Orders, privileges and conventions.

### 1258–1485

The story begins in 1258. After a period of disaster overseas and famine and unrest at home, Henry III and his advisers were in grave trouble.

A Parliament was summoned to meet at Oxford, of barons and prelates only. Peter de Montfort, perhaps a relation of Simon de Montfort, and later to die with him in the battle of Evesham, is said to have presided over it. He was an opponent of the Court.

This Parliament was called the 'Mad Parliament'. Laundy says that it owes its derogatory appellation to those whose abuses it sought to check. It managed to extort from the King a promise that Parliament should have direct control over the executive. A committee was appointed to prepare the plan of reform known as the Provisions of Oxford. The aims of the reformers were sound, but the machinery for carrying them out was too complicated. Nevertheless it was a considerable step forward in the political development of Parliament.

A bitter struggle continued between the King and Simon de Montfort, with his followers among the barons. The King was defeated at the battle of Lewes in 1264. Simon de Montfort's famous Parliament then met in the following year and introduced the principle of popular representation. This was an important landmark, the seven-hundredth anniversary of which was commemorated in 1965 in Westminster Hall.

Parliaments continued to be summoned. Points would be put to them by the King, and answers had somehow to be given. It was usually done by an informally chosen spokesman, who spoke on behalf of both the Lords and the Commons, or the Commons alone. On occasion there were fears that the chosen spokesman would not stand up to the King and dare to give him the agreed answer. A posse of fellow Members would therefore accompany him to see that he got it right.

These spokesmen also seem to have acted as presiding officers, but, although it is known that Parliaments were summoned on numerous occasions after 1258, there are no records of the names of these presiding officers until Sir William Thrussell in 1327. We do not know who presided over the Model Parliament of 1295, which established an assembly consisting of the three estates of the realm — the Lords, the Prelates and the Commons.

In 1326, Edward II was overthrown by his wife, Queen Isabella, from whom he had become estranged. She summoned a Parliament to meet at Westminster in January 1327. Its business was the deposition of the King. The

three estates agreed that the King should be deposed, and
that his son should succeed him as Edward III.

Sir William Thrussell announced this decision to
Edward II on behalf of Parliament. Edward III was
thus the first King to ascend the throne by the will of
Parliament.

Parliaments continued to be summoned during his
reign, and in most cases the names of the presiding officers
are known. In 1373 there was a crisis in the relations
between the throne and Parliament. The knights and
burgesses in Parliament refused a subsidy until they had
had a conference with the Lords to express their criticisms.
John of Gaunt was ruling in the King's name, and had
eventually to summon another Parliament in 1376. Peter
de la Mare presided. The Commons insisted on changes
at Court and in the membership of the Royal Council.
Even when they had their way over these matters, they
only granted to the King the tax on wool exports for three
months. They had gained new power and authority.

Sir Walter Hungerford presided over the next House of
Commons. For the first time, the title Speaker or its Latin
equivalent was given to the presiding officer.

De la Mare succeeded him in Richard II's first Parliament. His speech at its opening again showed the growing
influence of the Commons. De la Mare made proposals
for the administration of the State during the King's
minority. His petition relating to the membership of the
Council was accepted. During Richard's reign, other
precedents, relevant today, were set by Speakers on behalf
of the Commons. Speaker Pickering asserted the right of
free speech in the House. Guildesboro asserted the right of
the Commons to control public expenditure. Waldegrave
showed the reluctance to accept the office which has been
shown or simulated at almost every election since.

Richard II's last Speaker, Bussy, was one of the first to
deem it his duty to serve only the King and to keep the
Commons subservient. His loyalty was to the King not to

the Commons. He paid for it. When Henry IV deposed Richard II, Speaker Bussy was beheaded without trial.

But the tradition of a measure of independence on the part of the Speaker continued under Henry IV and Henry V, and until the outbreak of the Wars of the Roses.

Speaker Savage in 1404 demanded not only redress of grievances before granting money, but also immunity from arrest for debt or trespass. Speaker Tiptoft admonished the King upon his extravagances. To Speaker Thomas Chaucer the King conceded in 1407 that it was the Commons' right to be the initiators of financial measures. Under Speaker Walter Hungerford, the Commons were recognized in 1414 as legislators not just petitioners.

Thus some of the main principles of our parliamentary system slowly developed in the century and a half preceding the Wars of the Roses. But those bitter struggles, which lasted for over sixty years, halted the process. The influence of Parliament declined, and Speakers were chosen from the faction in power. Their mortality rate was high. The first casualty was William Tresham, a Yorkist, elected Speaker for the fourth time in 1449. The following year he was murdered by Lancastrians. His successor was William Oldfield, also a Yorkist. But the next Parliament of 1453 was Lancastrian. Oldfield was suspected of complicity in Jack Cade's rebellion, allegedly to further the Yorkist cause. Oldfield was found guilty, outlawed and attainted.

Thomas Thorpe, Speaker in the 1453 Parliament, was an immediate target when the Yorkists came back because he had seized some arms belonging to the Duke of York. He was sued for trespass; a £1,000 penalty, either damages or a fine, was imposed by the Court. He was committed to prison. The Commons declared this to be a breach of privilege and demanded his release. The Lords referred the matter to the Justices of the King's Bench. Sir John Fortescue, a great judge and constitutional lawyer, pronounced that it was for the High Court of Parliament and not for the Justices to decide on matters of privilege. Sir

2

John's view was not subsequently confirmed in practice. The tracing of the boundary between the competence of the Courts and the jurisdiction of either House on matters of privilege proved a highly complicated matter. Erskine May's treatise devotes a whole chapter to it.

In spite of the Commons' protest, Thorpe had to pay the £1,000. During the next Lancastrian upsurge in the Parliament of 1459, he no doubt enjoyed himself drawing up the bills of attainder against various Yorkists, including two ex-Speakers, Oldfield and John Wenlock.

John Wenlock was originally a Lancastrian, but was elected Speaker as a Yorkist in the 1455 Parliament. Some time after being attainted, he changed sides again, but to no avail. He was killed in battle in the Lancastrian defeat at Tewkesbury in 1471.

Thorpe was put in the Tower when the Yorkists came to power in 1460. When trying to escape in the guise of a monk, he was caught by the mob and beheaded by them.

The Lancastrian Parliament of 1459 had as Speaker Thomas Tresham, son of the Yorkist William Tresham, who had been murdered in 1450. Apparently Thomas was just as violent a Lancastrian as his father had been Yorkist. But he suffered a similar fate. He was captured at Tewkesbury in 1471 and beheaded.

The final casualty among Speakers in the Wars of the Roses was William Catesby, a devoted follower of Richard III. He fought with him at Bosworth, was taken prisoner and beheaded without trial.

### 1485–1603

Henry VII brought order once again to a very troubled kingdom. He was determined to rule in his own right. Civil war had reduced the number of temporal peers to twenty-nine. Henry created very few others, and so the Lords were virtually powerless. He ensured the subordination of the Commons in three ways. He summoned

Parliament rarely; he nominated the Speaker himself; and he achieved financial security independently of the House of Commons.

Henry's first Speaker was Thomas Lovell, a staunch friend who had been in exile with him, and his standard bearer at Bosworth. Lovell was an active promoter of Henry's financial methods. He was made Chancellor of the Exchequer for life, an appointment which today would certainly be regarded as a fate worse than death. He survived for thirty-nine years and died, like his master, enormously rich.

Two of Henry's Speakers were particularly diligent tax-gatherers—Empson, Speaker in 1491, and Dudley, Speaker in 1504. In their extortions they used every kind of fraud, oppression and cruelty, almost always outside the law. Morton, the Cardinal Archbishop of Canterbury, joined in. His claim to fame is 'Morton's fork', a tax which no one could escape. The big spenders had to pay on the grounds that they obviously could afford it. Those who lived quietly were caught on the grounds that they must be saving money, and so also could afford to pay up. The Star Chamber is another memorial of this period.

In the last thirteen years of Henry's reign Parliament is said to have met only once.

Henry VIII, who succeeded in 1509, thought it prudent that some popularity should be obtained for the Crown, and that a sop to public opinion was needed. Accordingly Empson and Dudley were convicted on a trumped-up charge of constructive treason and both were beheaded on Tower Hill in 1510.

Under Henry VIII, Edward VI and Mary, the Speakers continued for the most part to be the nominees of the Crown. Under Henry, there was one notable occupant of the Chair. Sir Thomas More was Speaker for four months in 1525. Cardinal Wolsey needed what was then a large sum of money for the French War, £800,000. It was to be raised by a tax of four shillings in the pound on every man's goods and land. Wolsey was probably instrumental in More's nomination, thinking that a Speaker of unusual quality was needed to get such a sum out of the Commons. Wolsey himself came down to the Commons in state, in his crimson ecclesiastical robes and with a considerable retinue. He demanded the money. The Commons listened to him sullenly. He commented on this 'marvelloys obstinate silence'.

More administered a rebuke in gentle but firm terms. On his knees, he replied that, although the Commons would willingly receive communications from outsiders and consider them, it was not according to precedent for the Commons to enter into discussion or debate with such individuals. Wolsey appears to have borne no malice for this rebuff, perhaps because More in the end persuaded the Commons to grant the money.

Eleven years later Rich, upon whose perjured evidence More had been convicted and executed, became Speaker. He was as evil as More had been good. Those who have written about the Speakership had difficulty in finding terms of opprobrium strong enough to describe him. Perjurer, torturer, time-server, fawning hypocrite, the most despicable man who ever sat in the Chair of the Commons, one of the meanest, most unscrupulous tools to the hands of Henry VIII, he became Lord Chancellor borne on the prostrate forms of those whom his infamies had brought to ruin.

As Dasent writes Rich had a part in the fall of Wolsey, the death of More, the deaths of Fisher, Cromwell, Wriothesley, the Protector Somerset, his brother Lord Seymour and the Duke of Northumberland. A monster in human shape, Rich stretched the rack with his own hands when Anne Askew was put to torture in the Tower.

The Speakers of this period were all subservient to the Crown. The difference between them was the degree of that subservience.

Under Elizabeth, more signs of the older independence

began to emerge. The Crown continued in effect to nominate the Speaker, although it was done slightly more indirectly. Ten Parliaments were summoned in her reign, which lasted forty-five years. Each time the Speaker was proposed by a Member of the Council or an Officer of the Household. In one case, that of Onslow in 1566, although he was proposed by the Comptroller, he sought to excuse himself on the ground that he was Solicitor-General and, in that capacity, had to attend the Lords. There was a vote, reputedly the first on the Speakership, and he was drafted by 82 votes to either 60 or 70 (the accounts vary), but the House decided that he might continue as Solicitor-General.

From Rich's time until the end of the seventeenth century, the Speakership has been described as being farmed by the Law. Five Speakers rose to the Woolsack as Chancellors or Keepers of the Great Seal. Three held it in commission while the Lord Chancellorship was vacant. Seven became Masters of the Rolls. More frequently still were the posts of Chief Justice of the Queen's or King's Bench, or of the Common Pleas, given to former Speakers. Barons of the Exchequer and Recorders of London are plentiful. Names and further details are to be found in Dasent's book. The emoluments of the Chair were low, but it was regarded as a stepping stone to high judicial office.

Queen Elizabeth got on tolerably well with her Parliaments despite differences of opinion. They annoyed her by pressing her to marry. They were more vindictive towards Mary Queen of Scots than she was herself. They constantly opposed her on questions of religious tolerance, being far more bigoted and against toleration. But she had immense prestige with them. While not consciously wishing to weaken her authority, they increasingly expressed their own opinions. The fact that leading Ministers such as Hatton and Cecil sat in the Commons and took part in debates, demonstrated the awareness of the Crown that it too had to argue its case.

There were some entertaining episodes. When the Queen asked Speaker Popham what had passed in the unproductive Parliament of 1581, he replied, 'If it please Your Majesty, seven weeks.' The Queen wrote to Speaker Puckering (1584–7) instructing him that no laws were to be passed in that Parliament, 'there being many more already than be well executed', which strikes a modern note.

Edward Coke, the eminent lawyer, was Speaker from 17th February to 10th April 1593. During those seven weeks, he appears to have been a docile servant of the Crown. It was to him that Puckering, by then Lord Keeper of the Great Seal, gave his remarkable definition of free speech, 'Your right of free speech is not to say anything that pleaseth you, and come out with what so ever may be your thought. Your right of free speech is the right of Aye or No.' This pronouncement from an ex-Speaker was evidently too much for Coke. He retired to his bed and the House could not meet for several days. When it did, it lasted a very short time. Coke returned to the House twenty-seven years later as champion of the liberties of the subject, but more of that in due course.

When his successor, Speaker Yelverton, was being proposed for the Chair by Knollys, Comptroller of the Queen's Household and a notoriously boring and long-winded speaker, the Commons 'hawked and spat', the contemporary method of shouting 'divide'. Yelverton him-self, once something of a radical, by 1597 had become what has been described as a 'mellow and cautious sexa-genarian'. He acknowledged his nomination with these words,

Neither from my person nor nature does this choice arise; for he that supplieth this place ought to be a man big and comely, stately and well spoken, his voice great, his carriage majestic, his nature haughty and his purse plentiful and heavy; but contrarily the stature of my body is small, myself not so well spoken, my voice low, my carriage lawyer like and of the common fashion, my nature soft and bashful, my purse thin, light and never yet plentiful.

## *1603–1728*

With the coming of the Stuarts, relations between the Crown and Commons grew steadily worse. Churchill in his *History of the English-Speaking Peoples* (1956) gives the reason,

> A society more complex than that of Tudor England was coming into being. Trade both foreign and internal was expanding. Coal mining and other industries were rapidly developing. Larger vested interests were in being. In the van stood London, ever glorious champion of freedom and progress; London with its thousands of lusty, free spoken prentices and its wealthy City guilds and companies. Outside London many of the landed gentry who supplied numerous Members to Parliament were acquiring close connections with new industry and trade. In these years the Commons were not so much seeking to legislate as trying to wring from the Crown admissions of ancient custom which would prevent before it was too late all this recent growth from falling under an autocratic grip. (vol. ii, p. 144)

As the relations between the monarch and the Commons changed, so did the role of the Speaker.

In James I's reign (1603–25) there were four Parliaments. The first lasted for seven years. It was the one which Guy Fawkes tried to blow up. The Speaker was Phelips of Somerset, who sought energetically to defend the privileges of the House of Commons. He reprimanded a Yeoman of the Guard for obstructing a Member. Over the election of a Member for Buckingham, the Commons won the right to be the lawful judges of their own returns.

They also established their immunity from arrest. Shirley, Member for Steyning in Sussex, had been imprisoned after his election but before Parliament met, for non-payment of a private debt. The Warden of the Fleet refused to release Shirley. The Warden was summoned to the Bar of the House and 'committed to the prison called Little Ease within the Tower'. He was later released on the King's intercession. He confessed his fault, and apologized on his knees at the Bar. This immunity from arrest was quickly defined by statute.

During this Parliament, rules were made to guide the Speaker in the conduct of debates, giving him power to deal with obstruction and irrelevance. Hissing was forbidden.

Meanwhile political tension grew. The King believed in the Divine Right of Kings. He acted accordingly in affairs large and small. He was increasingly opposed by men like Pym, who, as Churchill wrote, understood every move in the political game and would play it out remorselessly. James postponed calling his second Parliament as long as he could. It met in April 1614. Crewe was Speaker. He had served in only one previous Parliament, seventeen years before, and lacked the ability to manage the House. It passed no Bills and granted no Supply.

For the next seven years, James ruled without Parliament. His illegal exactions and other misdemeanours are well known. In 1616 he dismissed Coke as Chief Justice of the King's Bench. But in February 1620 he had to summon his third Parliament, when Coke returned to the House after an absence of twenty-seven years. Richardson was Speaker. He was ineffective. He tried to serve both the King and the Commons, on the whole siding with the King. He was more than once censured by the House. Members complained of his habit of leaving the Chair without the consent of the House to end debates embarrassing to the Crown. In June 1621 he adjourned the House at the King's command without putting the Question.

The House returned to face its first major constitutional battle with the Stuarts. The Commons petitioned against a Spanish marriage for Prince Charles, and in favour of war against Spain. The King rebuked them for meddling in affairs not their concern. The House petitioned again, asserting 'the ancient liberty of Parliament for freedom of speech, jurisdiction and just censure ... the same being our ancient and undoubted right and an inheritance received from our ancestors ...' The King replied, 'we cannot allow of the style, calling it your ancient and undoubted right and inheritance; but could rather have wished that ye had said that your privileges were derived from the grace and permission of our ancestors and us'.

This the Commons could not stand. They drew up the well-known protest that all affairs of state were proper subjects for counsel and debate in Parliament, and had it entered in the Journals. The King then sent for the Journals and tore out the leaf on which the protest was written.

The Parliament was dissolved in February 1622. James's last Parliament met two years later. Sir Thomas Crewe was Speaker. He did his best to oppose the enemies, now gathering strength, of an absolute monarchy. None the less a law was passed abolishing monopolies; the Lord Treasurer was impeached; and the Commons' right to appoint their own Commissioners for the management of moneys voted for Supply was accepted by the King.

These events dispose of the misconception that serious confrontation between Crown and Parliament began only with Charles I.

When Charles did come to the throne, matters went from bad to worse. His first Parliament lasted eight weeks and voted him only £140,000. His second was no better. His third, summoned in 1628, was the scene of a remarkable incident. The Commons, with men in it like Eliot, Pym, Digges, the aged Coke and Denzil Holles, prepared a Petition of Right, a declaration of the liberties of the subject.

The King was displeased and ordered them not to continue to debate the matter. There followed a temporary
truce, but soon the Commons were persevering in their
attacks upon Buckingham, the King's favourite. There
were also disputes over money and the King's High Church
policy.

Finch was the Speaker. His predecessor, Richardson,
had been told by Members, 'Mr. Speaker is but a servant
to the House, not a master, nor a master's mate.' He had
also been told to sit still. For Finch worse was to come.
When Eliot wished to raise some question, Finch refused
to put it on the ground that the King had commanded
the House to adjourn. On rising to adjourn the debate,
he was forcibly held back in his seat by Holles and others.
He was detained there until Eliot's motion had been
adopted. MacDonagh's more detailed and dramatic account
of this scene is well worth reading. As Laundy says, 'His
experience demonstrated conclusively that a Speaker who
served the Court interests had become an anachronism.'
Finch's tearful comment, 'I am not less the King's servant
for being yours', was no longer acceptable.

For eleven years Charles governed without Parliament.
He then summoned one which lasted only three weeks
and did not grant him the needed Supplies. A few months
later he tried again. It is believed that the election turned
on whether candidates were for or against the King. The
result was a crushing defeat for him. He had to face a
hostile House of Commons. It steadily reduced the power
of the Crown, to such an extent that, as the intentions
of Pym and his followers became the more obviously
revolutionary, a Royalist party began to form in the
House.

Charles, however, without consulting these supporters,
decided upon his disastrous confrontation. He decided to
impeach five of his principal opponents—Pym, Hampden,
Holles, Hazelrig and Strode. As the King entered Palace
Yard to arrest them, they slipped away into the Speaker's

garden and escaped down the river to the protection of the City.

Charles entered the Chamber, the only Sovereign who has ever crossed the Bar of the House. He went to the Chair and said to Speaker Lenthall, 'By your leave, Mr. Speaker, I must borrow your Chair a little.' Lenthall left the Chair and the King stepped up into it. He looked round but could not see any of the five Members. He then said to the House, 'in Cases of Treason no person hath a Privilege', and added that he must have them wherever he could find them. He added, some say good-humouredly, 'Well since I see all the birds are flown, I do expect from you that you shall send them unto me as soon as they return.'

The King then asked Lenthall whether any of them were in the House. Falling on his knees, Lenthall made his historic reply, 'May it please Your Majesty, I have neither eyes to see nor tongue to speak in this place, but as the House is pleased to direct me, whose servant I am here; and I humbly beg Your Majesty's pardon, that I cannot give any other answer than this to what Your Majesty is pleased to demand of me.'

The King went out of the House, 'which was in great disorder, and many Members cried out aloud so as he might hear them Privilege! Privilege! and forthwith adjourned.' All these quotations are from the record of Rushworth, the Clerk Assistant, which was taken down at the time.

Lenthall had made the position of the Speaker absolutely clear, and justly earned lasting fame. The Speaker was no longer to be regarded as a servant of the Crown. His first loyalty was to be to the Commons.

On 11th January, the five members returned triumphantly to Westminster. About six months later the Civil War broke out.

Apart from the week in 1647 when the mob broke into the House and Lenthall was forced to flee to Fairfax's headquarters, he remained Speaker. He was Speaker during

Pride's Purge, the occasion when Colonel Pride, supported by three regiments of soldiers, prevented any Members who were known to be in favour of coming to terms with the King from entering the Chamber. But Lenthall does not appear to have made any objection. He was in the Chair during the passage of the Bill enabling the House to try the King, and he put the Question on the resolution of January 1649, which defined the basis of the case against the King and asserted that he had been guilty of treason.

He continued as Speaker at the beginning of the Cromwellian era, and until Cromwell's forcible dismissal of the Rump in the Long Parliament in April 1653. The 'Barebones' Parliament followed, during which Rous was Speaker. But in the next Parliament, Lenthall was again elected Speaker, nominated by Cromwell. Cromwell dissolved this Parliament after a few months.

In the Parliament called in September 1656, Lenthall was not made Speaker, and he did not return to the Chair until Lambert's decision to recall the Rump of the Long Parliament in 1659. Except for a few days when he was ill, he continued in office until 16th March 1660 when the Long Parliament was finally dissolved.

Lenthall's ability to remain Speaker for sixteen years in all was a remarkable exercise in survival. Not surprisingly, much is alleged against him — petulance, greed, doubledealing, opportunism and finally, that at the trial of the regicides, when giving evidence, he appeared to depart from the principle which he had so courageously announced on that famous day in June 1642. Nor did he object to Pride's Purge.

Whatever substance there may be in these charges, he did maintain a certain continuity in the Speakership and he did contrive, whether by luck or good management, that it should remain a factor to be considered even by Cromwell and others, in the parliamentary vicissitudes after Charles's execution.

Charles II's first Parliament met in April 1660, although

he himself did not return until May, and lasted for eight months. Sir Harbottle Grimston was elected Speaker. It was called the Convention Parliament because it was not summoned by the King. It restored the monarchy, although insisting on its own privileges and on parliamentary control of Supply. It also confirmed Magna Charta, the Petition of Rights and all Acts embodying the rights and privileges of ordinary citizens.

Charles II's second Parliament lasted from May 1661 to January 1679. Edward Turnour was Speaker for the first ten years. The old relations between the Speaker and the Sovereign were restored. The Parliament was strongly Royalist, although there was a steady increase in opposition to the Government.

Sir Job Charlton's ten-day Speakership, ended by illness, was followed on 18th February 1673 by the election of Edward Seymour, the first non-lawyer for 150 years. He, too, regarded the Speaker's duty as primarily to serve the King. He was a strong Speaker and overbearing. MacDonagh refers to him as the most arrogant man who ever presided over the House of Commons. There is a well-known story about him. His coach broke down at Charing Cross. He ordered his attendants to stop the next coach to pass that way and commandeer it for his use. This was done. The indignant occupant resented being ejected. Seymour said, 'Sir, it is more proper for you to walk in the streets than the Speaker of the House of Commons.'

The Commons objected without success to Seymour being a Privy Councillor, on the grounds that it brought him too near the King. As in the days of Speaker Finch, the Commons also objected to his adjourning without any motion being passed by the House, either at the King's command or when he saw that things were developing awkwardly for the King.

There was an example of this in May 1677. The Commons opposed an alliance with France and favoured one with Holland. The King told them that this was an intolerable encroachment upon his prerogative, and directed that Parliament should be adjourned until July. The argument continued until the following February, Seymour sticking to his ground that the House must obey the King's command. The result was indecisive, the House adjourning without any resolution having been passed.

Charles II's third Parliament met in 1679. Meanwhile the King and Seymour had fallen out, it was said over a lady. The King refused to approve Seymour when the Commons again chose him, the first and last time I think that the Sovereign's approval has been withheld. The Commons bitterly resented Charles's action. Grimston, a former Speaker, argued that the Sovereign's approval was only a formality, and that the choice must be that of the Commons.

A tussle between the King and the Commons ensued. There were representations and discussions. The King wanted Sir Thomas Meres. The Commons would not have him. The King would not give way, and in the end a compromise candidate, Sir William Gregory, was elected and approved by the King.

The 1680 general election went against the Court. William Williams was chosen Speaker. He had been a critic of the King's ordering of the adjournment of the House in Seymour's time. He was a Whig, Member for Chester and the first Welshman to occupy the Chair. As a known radical he could not bring himself to be other than frank on his selection. To the Commons he said,

Gentlemen it were vanity in me by argument from weakness and unfitness to disable myself for your service in this Chair at this time. The unanimous voice of the House calling me to this place precludes me, and leaves me without excuse. Whom the Commons have elected for this trust is to be supposed worthy and fit for it: wherefore I must acquiesce in your commands.

To the King he said (words from which I quoted on my own re-election in October 1974),

> I am set in the first station of your Commons for trust and quality, an high and slippery place. It requires a steady head and a well poised body in him that will stand firm there. Uprightness is the safe posture and best policy, and shall be mine in this place, guarded with this opinion—that Your Majesty's service in this trust is one and the same with the service of the Commons, and that they are no more to be divided than your crown and sceptre.

For all his professions, Williams is said to have been as prejudiced in favour of the Whigs as most of his predecessors had been loyal to the Sovereign.

Charles came into conflict with the House over the succession. The Commons wished to exclude his brother James, Duke of York, from the succession. He dissolved Parliament, and summoned another one to meet at Oxford, where he thought the atmosphere would be more favourable. However, the Commons were no more compliant, so the King dissolved Parliament after a week and ruled for the last two years of his life without one.

James II succeeded in 1685. The only Parliament of his reign was strongly Tory. The Crown nominated Sir John Trevor, another Welshman and member for Denbigh, as Speaker. He was proposed by a Secretary of State and unanimously elected. For the first time the King's speech stating the reasons for calling the Parliament was not made until after the Speaker's election. This precedent has been followed ever since.

Trevor had a bad squint. It is said that when he bowed to call a member, one got up on each side of the House; hence the practice of calling members by name or pointing with the finger. I do not know whether this is true or not.

James II fled in 1688. Once again the country was

without a Sovereign. Another Convention Parliament was summoned, and William and Mary were installed as monarchs in the same way that Charles II had been pronounced King in 1660. On each occasion there was no Sovereign to call the Parliament and approve the Speaker. Henry Powle was Speaker of this Parliament for the fortnight or so which it lasted.

Trevor was elected Speaker again in the next Parliament, called in 1690, and continued for five years. He was then discovered in an act of corruption. He took 1,000 guineas from the City to help get through rather a good Bill in favour of certain orphans. His acceptance of this gratuity was, on 12th March 1695, declared to be a high crime and misdemeanour. He resigned ostensibly on the ground of illness, and was expelled from the House on 16th March. He was not deprived of his position as Master of the Rolls, but continued to sit as a judge for a further 20 years, establishing, it is said, a high reputation for ability and uprightness.

One of the Acts passed early in the reign of William and Mary established the Speaker's precedence as the First Commoner in the land. He ranked first after the peers. This continued until 1919, when on the initiative of Speaker Lowther, the Speaker was put ahead of the majority of peers (the new order being as set out on page 19). The Speaker, however, is no longer the First Commoner, because since 1919 the Prime Minister has always been a Commoner, and from time to time the Lord President of the Council has also sat in the Commons. However, the error of still describing the Speaker as the First Commoner persists: no less a person than Sir Winston Churchill, when congratulating Speaker Clifton Brown on his re-election in August 1945, referred to him maintaining the reputation of the First Commoner in England.

After Trevor's expulsion, the Court's nominee was Sir Thomas Littleton, a Whig. The Tory majority in the Commons chose instead Paul Foley, and he was elected.

This was a significant change. The Speaker was no longer to be a nominee of the Crown, but rather, as the party system developed, of the majority of the House of Commons. He was also expected to be a partisan and to manage the Commons in the interests of his party. With the notable exception of Arthur Onslow and of one or two others, the Speakership became a stepping stone not to the Bench, as it had been, but to high political office.

The election in 1701 of that outstanding personality, Robert Harley, confirmed this new practice. After four years as Speaker, he became a Secretary of State, then Chancellor of the Exchequer and later, as Lord Oxford, was Lord Treasurer, in effect Prime Minister.

None of Harley's immediate successors was as successful a Speaker as he, or attained such political eminence. But, with one exception, all did well.

John Smith, Speaker from 1705 to 1708 and a Whig, became Chancellor of the Exchequer in 1708. Sir Richard Onslow, Speaker from 1708 to 1710, also a Whig, became Chancellor of the Exchequer in 1714. Bromley, a Tory, was elected Speaker when the Tories won the 1710 Election. He later became a Secretary of State. Sir Spencer Compton, a Whig, after his Party's victory in 1715 was Speaker for twelve years. A favourite of George II, he ultimately became First Lord of the Treasury in 1742, again in effect Prime Minister.

## 1728–1839

At last in 1728, some ninety years after Lenthall's first election, a Speaker was chosen who achieved fame and eminence through his conduct of the Speakership. He was Arthur Onslow. Elected to the House eight years before, he became Speaker at the age of thirty-six and continued for thirty-three years. He saw the development of Cabinet Government coupled with ministerial responsibility to Parliament. He saw the elder Pitt enter the House; he

saw the rise of the newspaper press; he saw Government and
Opposition supporters begin to sit on opposite sides of the
Chamber; he ensured great improvements in the keeping of
official records.

His distinction as Speaker, however, lay in none of these
things. He must be accounted a great Speaker, perhaps the
greatest of all, because he saw that the survival of Parliament as a reputable institution depended on the independence and impartiality of the Chair. He recognized
that the Chair itself must set the example in the maintenance
of high standards. In 1742 he resigned the lucrative post of
Treasurer of the Navy so that it could not be said that he
held the Speakership for reasons of personal financial gain.
His adherence to procedural details of the utmost triviality,
seemed to many overdone. He was a stickler for good
manners in the House, and proper respect for the Chair.
To some he seemed obsessed with pomp and pageantry.
He was said not to have had a sense of humour. Whatever
truth or lack of it there is in all this, he laid the foundations
for the Speakership as we now know it, and he described
these foundations in his valedictory address, 'When I began
my duty here, I set out with a resolution and promise to
the House, to be impartial in everything, and to show
respect to everybody. The first I know I have done: it is
the only merit I can assume. If I have failed in the other,
it was unwillingly, it was inadvertently,' and he ended,
' ... my daily prayer will be ... that the freedom, the dignity
and authority of this House may be perpetual.' As Laundy
says, 'He ennobled the Speakership and set for it an
imperishable tradition.'

After Arthur Onslow, the Speakership reverted. Cust
(1761–70) lacked authority and the physical strength to
sustain the trials and tribulations brought upon him by
John Wilkes. They involved many parliamentary storms.
Speaker Cust's health failed and he died in office at the age
of fifty-one.

In the ensuing election for Speaker, Fletcher Norton

(1770–80), the Tory nominee, beat the Whig by 237 votes to 121. According to all accounts, he was an unattractive, ill-mannered, offensive person. Although he won some support for his confrontation with George III in 1777 over Supply, the House never liked him.

His successor, Charles Wolfran Cornwall (1780–89) was a Tory. He is remembered chiefly for his habit of relieving the tedium of the Chair with copious draughts of porter. As Dasent writes, 'the oratorical triumphs of Pitt and Fox, the thunder of Burke, the lightning like flashes of Sheridan's wit' could not keep the Speaker from falling asleep in his Chair. He was the last Bencher of Gray's Inn before myself to be Speaker. He died in office. 'Never', wrote Wraxall, 'was any man in a public situation less regretted or sooner forgotten.'

Grenville was elected Speaker on 5th January 1789 at the age of twenty-nine, the nominee of his cousin William Pitt the younger, who had become Prime Minister at the age of twenty-three. Grenville then became Home Secretary on 5th June 1789 and resigned the Speakership. He was Foreign Secretary from 1791 to 1801, and Prime Minister from 1806 to 1807.

Grenville was succeeded by Addington. His father had been the regular medical attendant of Pitt's father, the famous and, until his declining years, robust Lord Chatham. He was only thirty-two, and remained in the Chair for nearly twelve years—fair, courteous and generally respected, but posterity has remembered him for Canning's couplet

> Pitt is to Addington
> As London is to Paddington

Fortescue is reputed to have written of him, 'He possesses the sober mediocrity which qualifies a man for the position of Speaker.' Some say that the emphasis should be put on the epithet sober, in that age of the two-bottle men. That mediocrity was meant to be the operative word is rather confirmed by Lord Spencer in 1834. When Spring Rice was a candidate for the Speakership in that year, Spencer wrote to him, 'I am surprised, I own, that you should choose to lower yourself to so fameless an office ... Addington and Abbot made better Speakers than Sutton because they had less sense, and Lord Grenville made a much worse one, I believe, because he had more.'

Poor Addington, he became Prime Minister in 1801, Lord President of the Council in 1805 and Home Secretary in 1812. It was Canning again who said of him 'Addington is like the chicken pox or the measles. Ministers are bound to have him at least once in their lives.'

As to the 'famelessness' and mediocrity of Speakers, rebuttal had to await the advent of Shaw-Lefevre and the Victorian Speakers who followed him.

Charles Abbot was Speaker from February 1802 to June 1817. Charles Manners-Sutton was Speaker from June 1817 to December 1834. They were what Laundy describes as the last of the partisan Speakers. It was not disputed that they were fair when in the Chair, but as Tories each remained influential while Speaker in the councils of their Party.

In his speech at the Bar of the House of Lords on the prorogation of the session in 1813 (a speech which mercifully is no longer expected of the Speaker), Abbot expressed himself as strongly opposed to the removal of Roman Catholic disabilities.

This brought down on his head a vote of censure which, although defeated in the division lobby, left its mark. Thus Charles Manners-Sutton, who also intervened in debate on the same contentious subject, felt obliged to apologize to the House for his intrusion. He too was a strong party man; he was offered the Home Secretaryship and mentioned as a possible Prime Minister even while Speaker.

Dismayed by the passing of the Reform Bill of 1832, Manners-Sutton wished to retire. The Whips, however, fearing that only an experienced Speaker could curb the radical element in the newly reformed House of Commons, prevailed on him to remain. He was still Speaker, therefore, when fire destroyed the Houses of Parliament and the Speaker's House in 1834.

William IV dismissed the Whigs in 1834, and the Tories took office under Sir Robert Peel. But the Whigs won the ensuing election. Peel decided to face a hostile House of Commons as Prime Minister. His first action was to support Manners-Sutton for Speaker against Abercromby, the candidate of the Whigs. Although Manners-Sutton had been chosen Speaker on seven previous occasions, this time he was defeated by 316 votes to 306.

He remained a member of the House for a few weeks after this defeat; then went to the Lords. I have been told that the only time he was seen to smile in the Chair was when a rat ran across the floor of the House.

Abercromby was Speaker for four years. Although he was highly thought of by the officials of the House, Mac-Donagh describes it as a disappointing Speakership. Disraeli was elected to the House for the first time in 1837 and described in caustic terms, to his sister Sarah, Abercromby's re-election, 'Shaw-Lefevre proposed, and Strutt of Derby seconded, Abercromby. Both were brief, the first commonplace, the second commonplace and coarse; all was tame. Peel said a little, very well. Then Abercromby, who looked like an old laundress, mumbled and moaned some dullness, and was then carried to the chair and said a little more amid a faint, dull cheer.'

## 1839–1970

I now come to the twelve Speakers whose portraits adorned the walls of my large dining-room in Speaker's House. I served under four of them, and met a fifth during the last War. In each case I have become familiar not only with their portraits but also their conduct of the Speakership.

Abercromby resigned and was succeeded by Shaw-

Lefevre (1839–57). He was an undoubted success, and is said to have controlled the House admirably. When he had to rule and there was no precedent, he made one, adding so as to prevent further discussion 'according to the well-known practice of the House'. If anyone then questioned the ruling, he would say firmly, 'Order, Order, the point is already disposed of.' Considerable reforms in procedure were made in his time to expedite business. Following the report of a Select Committee a Deputy Speaker was appointed in 1853.

He was succeeded by Denison (1857–72). He too did well, although he was not quite as firm as Shaw-Lefevre. He was the last Speaker to speak and vote in Committee. He was also the last Speaker to have to deal with the possibility of a duel between two members. He upheld the rights of the Commons against encroachments by the Lords. His views on the Speaker's casting vote have led to the modern practice. He deprecated questions being submitted to the Speaker as a device for questioning Ministers. As Laundy puts it, 'Arthur Onslow had originated the modern conception of the Speakership, and Shaw-Lefevre had restored it. Denison's achievement lay in its consolidation.' He also had to cope with the first indications of real trouble from Irish members.

Brand, the next Speaker (1872–84), had been Liberal Chief Whip. The wisdom of selecting him was questioned on that ground. However he soon proved himself. He had the doubtful privilege of being in the Chair during times of unparalleled difficulty and disorder. There was no way to closure debates, and the Irish Nationalists, feeling no loyalty to Parliament, perceived that this could be used to their advantage.

Brand began by being conciliatory. Then he ruled that obstruction was a contempt of the House. In 1880 a Standing Order was approved providing for the suspension of any member named by the Speaker for wilfully obstructing the business of the House.

In January 1881 the matter came to a head. At 4 p.m.
on the 31st, discussion of the Coercion Bill began. There
followed the longest sitting which the House had ever
known. It continued for 41½ hours. Then at 9 a.m. on
1st February, Brand announced his intention of putting
the Question at once. This bold step, although of course
opposed by the Irish, was widely approved. At noon the
next day a question was put challenging the Speaker's
conduct. 'I answered', Brand says, 'on the spur of the
moment that I had acted on my own responsibility, and
from a sense of duty to the House. I never heard such loud
and protracted cheering, none cheering more loudly than
Gladstone.' Gladstone reported to the Queen, 'The Speaker's
firmness in mind, his suavity in manner, his unwearied
patience, his incomparable temper, under a thousand
provocations, have rendered possible a really important
result.'

A new Standing Order was later introduced providing
for the suspension of the regular order of business and giving
the Speaker power to substitute such rules as he thought
fit. The suspension of the regular order of business had to
be carried by the House itself with a three to one majority
in a House of at least three hundred members.

There was a feeling at the time that this Standing Order
gave the Speaker too much power. In the following six
years the House felt its way towards the rules which,
broadly speaking, prevail today. The Speaker was given
authority to refuse dilatory motions, to refuse a division
unnecessarily claimed and to direct a member to cease
speaking on the ground of irrelevance or tedious repetition.
Although at first the initiative over the closure was left
with the Chair, in 1887 it was transferred to the House,
the moving of the motion whether by the Government or
anyone else remaining subject to the Speaker's approval.

Some means of closuring debates would have been bound
to come in due course, but Brand certainly deserves great
credit for his courage and judgment. It is arguable whether

he showed the same skill in his handling of the prolonged tensions created by Bradlaugh's refusal to take the oath, after his election for Northampton.

Peel (1884–95) succeeded Brand. He is said to have been a most impressive and powerful Speaker. His speeches both on taking and leaving the Speakership made a profound impact on the House. He was by nature a grave and austere man. As Laundy says, the blind eye and the deaf ear had no place in his equipment. He exercised iron control over debate, and would tolerate no argument over his rulings. He was always tense and alert, or as an Irish Member complained 'on the pounce'. MacDonagh, who saw him in action, thought that at times he was too impulsive and authoritative. MacDonagh suspected that Peel suffered much pain from a varicose vein in his leg, and that that led to occasional loss of temper. Nevertheless he was an outstanding Speaker.

During his time, the Irish Nationalists, although their powers to obstruct were curtailed, showed no sign of being subdued. It was also during Peel's time that the initiative over the closure rightly passed from the Chair to the House.

When Peel resigned there was trouble about a successor. The last five Speakers had been Liberals. The Liberals were in political trouble and expected to lose the election, which would not be long delayed. They were willing to offer it to a Liberal Unionist, Courtney, but he was not acceptable to his own side. A further complication was that Sir Henry Campbell-Bannerman very much wanted to be Speaker. He had been nearly thirty years in the House and Chief Secretary for Ireland and Secretary of State for War. He had been warned about his health and was attracted by the prospect of not having to make speeches during the recesses. It was clear that his Party would lose the election and might have a long time before it in Opposition. The Conservatives would have accepted him as Speaker.

But Campbell-Bannerman's colleagues were very much against the idea. He was said to be the only one on speaking terms with all of them. For once Rosebery, the Prime Minister, and Harcourt, the Leader in the Commons, were agreed and Campbell-Bannerman reluctantly acquiesced. Rosebery wrote saying how glad he was that a man of real ability was not to be 'embedded in that pompous tomb', echoes of Earl Spencer to Spring Rice!

Eventually another Liberal, Gully (1895–1905), became Speaker. The Conservatives were not consulted about his nomination, and bitterly opposed it. His seat at Carlisle was marginal and he was being unfairly imposed upon them; therefore they ran a rival candidate for the Speakership. Gully had a majority in the House of only eleven votes.

The Conservatives won their expected victory in the general election, but, although they opposed Gully in his constituency, his majority, against the trend, was substantially increased. The Conservatives themselves proposed his re-election as Speaker.

This precedent of a Party supporting the re-election of a Speaker drawn from an opposing Party was followed by the Liberals in the case of Speaker Lowther in 1906, by Labour in 1945 with Speaker Clifton Brown, in 1970 by the Conservatives with Speaker King, and by Labour with myself in March and October 1974.

Gully was a competent Speaker but restrictive. He would not allow supplementary questions; his interpretation of Standing Orders was strict. On procedural matters he was good, and never faulted. His worst day, however, was in 1901. The Irish Members had created a row. Some of them had been named, suspended and ordered to withdraw. They physically resisted efforts by the Messengers to remove them, and with success. Gully sent for a body of policemen to reinforce the Messengers. The Irish Members were removed but it was felt that Gully had lost prestige. He never fully recovered his authority.

Lowther (1905–21) was the first Conservative to be elected Speaker since Manners-Sutton in 1833. He was unopposed in the 1905 general election: as hounds happened to be meeting on nomination day, he handed in his papers clad in his hunting pink. Laundy writes warmly of him, 'by his good humour, kindliness and the warmth of his personality, he removed himself from the frosty plane of remoteness wherein his predecessors had tended to dwell.'

He had much with which to contend—the influx of new Members after the Liberal landslide of 1905, the constitutional crisis following the Lords' rejection of the 1909 Budget, the Parliament Act of 1911, the savage controversy over Irish Home Rule, the First World War, his Speaker's Conference, and the enfranchisement of women. In addition to deep divisions on policy, there was acute personal hostility both in and out of the House. Old friends would barely speak. A Conservative would not accept a dinner invitation if a Liberal had also been invited. Speaker Lowther certainly had a difficult time.

Laundy's view of his friendliness was not entirely shared by all those who served in the House under his Speakership. Sir Colin Coote, elected for the Isle of Ely in 1916, has said to me, 'We new and infant Members, though survivors of the Great War, were terrified of him. He could be extremely frosty to people he did not like', and went on to describe how on one occasion Lowther stopped even the redoubtable and voluble Commander Kenworthy in his tracks.

I met him in Suffolk in 1940, then aged about eighty-five, clear of mind and showing all the qualities to which Laundy referred. I asked him which was the greatest Parliamentarian whom he had known during his thirty-seven years of membership. He replied without hesitation 'Asquith'.

From time to time there is argument about whether it is a good thing that the Speaker should first have been Deputy Speaker and Chairman of Ways and Means. Lowther, Whitley (1921–8), Clifton Brown (1943–51), King (1965–71), and the present Speaker were all Deputy

Speakers and Chairmen of Ways and Means. FitzRoy (1928–43) had been Deputy Chairman of Ways and Means. Morrison (1951–9), Hylton-Foster (1959–65) and I myself (1971–6) had not held these offices. There is an advantage in the Speaker having had previous experience in the Chair, but it would be a mistake for it to be an automatic reversion.

It will be clear from this long record that the authority of the House of Commons vis-à-vis the Sovereign and the House of Lords has grown gradually and, except for parts of the fifteenth and sixteenth centuries, almost continuously. In 1949 the delaying power of the House of Lords was further curtailed. They can now hold up a Bill only for one Session, instead of for two as laid down by the Parliament Act of 1911. There has been a relaxation in ceremonial. Under the Royal Assent Act 1967, the Commons no longer have to attend the bar of the House of Lords to hear the Royal Assent signified in the ancient Norman French form 'La Reyne le veult'. It can be announced from the Chair by the Speaker.

# III

# Powers of the Speaker

The acceptance of the impartiality of the Speaker during Shaw-Lefevre's period of office (1839–57) has resulted in his being entrusted by the Commons, over the last one hundred and twenty-five years or so, with more and more powers, discretions and responsibilities. His independent status is recognized by his salary being a charge on the Consolidated Fund and so not subject to the need for an annual vote. He ceases to belong to a political party on his election to the Chair. At subsequent general elections, he stands as 'The Speaker seeking re-election'. He exercises his vote in the House only in the event of a tie, and then according to well-established principles.

## Maintenance of Order

His first duty nowadays is to preserve the order and dignity of proceedings in the House. He has wide powers. He can call Members to order for the use of unparliamentary language, for unbecoming behaviour, for irrelevance and for tedious repetition. He can order Members to resume their seats, or to withdraw a word or a phrase. In accordance with Standing Orders, he can order a Member to leave the Chamber. If a Member does not obey him, he can 'name' that Member, whereupon the suspension of the Member from the service of the House is moved by the

Leader of the House or the senior Minister present. If the Member does not leave the House, he can be removed forcibly by the Doorkeepers or Messengers acting under the Serjeant at Arms, at the order of the Speaker.

If grave disorder arises in the House the Speaker has power under the Standing Orders to adjourn the House or to suspend the sitting for a stated period. By custom he also has power to suspend the sitting informally if he considers that this would assist the transaction of business or if an emergency, such as the illness of a Member in the Chamber, requires it.

These are stringent powers. Presidents of other Assemblies used to tell me how much they envied them. But in practice the Speaker has to be circumspect as to the extent to which he uses them. During my five years I did not ever 'name' a Member, but on several occasions I had to suspend the sitting.

There are perennial attempts to get round the Standing Orders or the practice of the House. The Speaker constantly has to say that he is not responsible for the content of a ministerial answer, that he does not decide whether a statement should be made, how questions should be grouped for answer, or which Minister should answer. He has to be firm with Members who try to raise, as points of order, what are essentially arguments on the merits of a case.

Erskine May asserts rather optimistically that 'Good temper and moderation are the characteristics of Parliamentary language', but the House of Commons has always been a lively place. Lord Ullswater, formerly Speaker Lowther, wrote in his memoirs, 'Among the most fruitful sources of disorder are the unmannerly interruptions and offensive personalities which I regret to think have much increased in the half century of public life of which I have experience.' He retired in 1921.

I doubt very much whether behaviour became worse in the thirty years or so of my membership, although age tends to make one a 'laudator temporis acti' (a praiser of times gone by). It is true that in the 1945–50 Parliament, relations between those on the front benches who had served together in the wartime coalition, were cordial. As for the rest of us, I quote from a letter which I wrote to my parents about what happened on 5th April 1949. I have added in brackets the Party to which a Member named belonged.

We had a first class row last night. Strachey (Labour) was making a very bad speech when Martin Lindsay (Conservative) called him an ex-Fascist. That infuriated the Socialists. Paton (Labour) described it as a lying accusation. Hogg (Conservative) lost his temper with the Deputy Speaker because he was not making Paton withdraw. Strachey's last words were drowned in hubbub.

After the question was put, there were nearly some free fights. Mrs. Manning (Labour) wanted to hit Hinchingbrooke (Conservative). The Government Chief Whip had to push Lindsay out of the way of enraged comrades. Beverley Baxter (Conservative) thought that he was manhandling Lindsay, whereupon a Socialist hit Baxter in the face. Waldron Smithers (Conservative) who was well away, tried to push into the middle of the scrum and shoved Lady Davidson (Conservative) out of the way, so she turned on him. He told her to shut her b—— mouth, so that was a private Conservative row. Eddie Winterton (Conservative and Father of the House) was delighted and said it was quite like old times when the Irish Nationalists were here. Mrs. Braddock (Labour) kept up a chant of 'hooligans'.

This was 1949 but unmannerly interruptions and offensive personalities have certainly continued since.

As to behaviour in the Chamber, a lady told me only

recently how horrified she had been to visit the House of Commons before the Second World War and see a well-known lady Member sit there with her feet up filing her finger-nails, without reproof from anyone.

Speakers have consistently had to rebuke Members for sedentary interruptions, or for too lengthy supplementary questions or interventions. Frequently Members indulge in conversation with one another, sometimes to such an extent that the speaker cannot be heard. More than once I had to remind the House of Speaker Coke's admonition in 1593, when he saw some Members whispering together, that it was not the manner of the House that any should whisper or talk secretly 'for here only public speeches are to be used'.

All this I tried to do with 'good temper and moderation'. Where I had to be very firm was over the use of unparliamentary language. Erskine May contains a list of words or phrases disallowed over the years, but there is not always time to refer to it.

I tried to draw a distinction between an attack on a man personally and for his personal character and an attack upon him for his political statements or opinions. A Minister once at the end of a long day shouted at his opposite number 'Bloody humbug'. I intervened to say that if that description was meant to apply to the Member concerned it was out of order. If it applied to his arguments, I deprecated the epithet but the noun was not out of order.

In 1973 I was asked to rule whether the expression 'a pack of lies' was in order. It had been used by the then Chancellor of the Exchequer on 7th November 1972 from a sedentary position, and repeated by him on 8th November when on his feet. The then Leader of the Opposition used it on 10th April 1973. On none of these occasions was any complaint made. I arranged however to be asked for a ruling.

I said that since 1921, the Chair had ordered the following words to be withdrawn — 'a lie', 'that's a lie', 'he is lying',

'liar', 'deceiving', 'lied to the House', 'deliberately mis-
leading', 'deliberately misled', 'a damn lie'. I continued,

> As to whether the Chair should intervene without a
> request for a ruling is a matter of judgment. In none of
> the three cases of the use of the words 'a pack of lies'
> was I asked for a ruling. Indeed in the first instance,
> I do not think that I heard the remark. Nevertheless
> I have come to the conclusion that I was at fault on the
> second and third occasions, and should have inter-
> vened to rule the expression as unparliamentary and
> I certainly intend to do so in the future if I hear it
> repeated. This will also apply to similar allegations of
> deliberate untruthfulness.

Frequently the word 'lie' is used in the heat of the
moment. I found it wise for me to intervene rather slowly.
I would say after a preamble that it was a word which I
was not permitted to allow, and that I was sure the Member
would think of some other way of making his point. By
doing it slowly, I gave the Member time to recover his
temper.

Phrases disallowed in my time were 'grossly deceived the
House', 'bloody hypocrite', 'bloody twister'. Although
asked to do so, I did not disallow an accusation of filibustering, or one that a Member was a Communist.

Occasionally there would be periods of prolonged tension
and then a sudden storm. At the end of the Second Reading
debate on the Bill to enable the United Kingdom to join
the E.E.C., on 17th February 1972, five Liberals voted
with the Conservatives and there was a majority for the
Government of eight. A popular Labour Member went
over to the Liberal bench and in an outburst of temper
either made some offensive remark or indulged in a minor
degree of physical contact. I could not see what happened.
The noise was so great that I would have had to suspend
the sitting I had wanted to pursue the matter that night.

In fact the Member concerned made an apology to the House a day or two later, which was willingly accepted.

There are however times when disorder assumes more serious proportions. My first experience of this came very quickly. On 18th and 19th January 1971, just over a week after my election as Speaker, the Committee Stage of the bitterly contested Industrial Relations Bill was taken on the floor of the House. Whitelaw, the Leader of the House, announced in reply to the routine question about the business for the following week, that Monday the 25th would be devoted to consideration of a time table motion on that Bill. This is a motion fixing a time by which consideration of a Bill must be completed. A committee on which the major parties are both represented divides up the total time allotted between the various parts of the Bill, grouping the clauses and schedules. Discussion must cease at the time fixed. It is colloquially called the guillotine because a procedural guillotine falls and cuts off further debate. That created uproar. Over twenty columns of *Hansard*, the Official Report, were needed to print the questions, answers, points of order on that item, and on the business for the rest of the following week. In time, it took sixty-five minutes. I had to intervene over twenty-five times. It was a baptism of fire for what was to come on the following Monday.

On that day, the Government guillotine motion was debated. It followed the conventional pattern of all debates on guillotine motions, whichever Party is in power. The spokesman for the Government of the day says that it is a sensible step to ensure proper discussion of an important measure, such discussion being currently frustrated by the delaying tactics in committee of the Opposition of the day. The Opposition spokesman then says that the motion is a monstrous interference with freedom of debate and a step on the path to dictatorship and the destruction of parliamentary institutions. I have listened to many such debates. If one shut one's eyes, one would not be able to

3

tell which Party was proposing or opposing. Following a recommendation of the Procedure Committee, the length of this kind of debate has been limited to three hours, by Standing Order No. 44.

On 25th January, however, it went on all day and was quiet compared with the previous Thursday, although expectation of trouble continued. I was in the Chair for the opening speeches, returned for an hour and a half or so in the middle of the debate, and then came back at 9 p.m. for the final speeches. Just before I returned, I was told that certain members of the Opposition were bent on trouble. I discussed with my advisers the possibilities. John Beckett in 1930 had seized the Mace and tried to carry it out of the Chamber. Was it to be that? In earlier days, the Clydesiders had had to be prised out of their seats one by one by Doorkeepers under the control of the Serjeant at Arms acting on the Speaker's orders, and conducted from the Chamber. Was it to be that? Would they try to remove me forcibly from the Chair, with the shade of Charles I looking on benignly? Would they try to prevent the tellers announcing the result of the division?

I had been Speaker for exactly thirteen days. I went back into the Chair in doubt as to what would happen, but, I admit, with a certain feeling of excitement and indeed exhilaration. It was as if one were back at school before an important match, anxious for fear one would let the side down but keyed up all the same.

Robert Carr, the Minister of Labour, began his summing up at 9.30 p.m. Almost at once there was trouble. One Labour Member sought to intervene about ten times. Then I began to notice some of the rowdier elements on the Opposition side gradually infiltrating towards seats on the benches by the middle gangway.

At about 9.50 p.m., while Carr was still speaking, they crowded out on to the floor of the House, and stood, some sixty of them, in a solid phalanx, beyond the Table, shouting at me, and making it impossible for the Minister to be heard.

What transpired is for all to read in the Official Report,

9.50 p.m.

*Mr. Speaker*: Order (interruption). Order. If honourable members defy the Chair (interruption). Order. Throughout the debate I have allowed opportunities for a reasonable expression of opinion on the Motion. The conduct of honourable Members is very disorderly (interruption). Order. This is getting almost as boring as a standing ovation (interruption). I really must ask honourable members (interruption). I understand their strength of feeling, but I must ask honourable members to leave the front of the Table and return to their seats (interruption). If honourable members persist in challenging the authority of the Chair in this way, I shall suspend the sitting for 15 minutes.

Suspended it was. I left the Chamber and returned to Speaker's House.

The problem was what to do next, when the sitting was resumed at 10.05 p.m. I knew what the demonstrators wanted. If I 'named' them one by one, there would have to be a motion moved by the Leader of the House to suspend the member named. A division could take place upon it. The rate of progress would be very slow. It might take days for the Government to get their motion. Eric Heffer's book* makes it clear that this was their purpose.

A possible answer would have been to name them en bloc, but I doubted whether the House would stand for that, at all events until many hours had been spent on points of order and on suspending individual members.

Another possibility was that if they continued to demonstrate I should continue to suspend for periods of fifteen

* *The Class Struggle in Parliament* (1973).

minutes. The Clerk thought that when I had done that four or five times, the demonstrators would become bored and throw in their hands. I had my doubts.

What I decided to do was to call at once the Prime Minister's motion on the Order Paper to suspend the Ten O'clock Rule and allow the debate to continue after 10 p.m. Under the Standing Orders, a debate has to end at 10 p.m., unless this rule has been suspended. The suspension can be for a limited time or indefinitely. In this case the motion was for an indefinite suspension.

I returned to the House at 10.05 p.m. The sixty or so demonstrators had resumed their positions in front of the Table. I thought most of them looked a little shamefaced, but there was no doubt about their intentions.

Accordingly, I at once called the Prime Minister. The Chief Whip nodded, and amid a crescendo of noise from in front of me, I put the Question that the Ten O'clock Rule be suspended. The Government side shouted 'aye' and the Opposition 'noe'. I cried,' Clear the lobby', and called for a division.

This left the crowd in front of me completely disconcerted. During a division, members wander about in the Chamber, and there was no point in the demonstrators staying where they were, particularly as they had to vote. Charles Loughlin, the Labour Member for West Gloucestershire, made a last despairing effort and raised a point of order. During a division this has to be done seated and covered, i.e., with a hat on. One of those old-fashioned expanding opera hats is kept readily available for the covering. His point was that the Ten O'clock Motion should have been put at 10 p.m. whereas I had put it at 10.10 p.m., therefore it was out of order. I ruled that I had put it at the earliest possible moment after 10 p.m. and therefore it was in order. It was carried by 308 votes to 276, and the first Opposition amendment was at once called.

That was the end of that, except for a slightly bizarre

sequel. One distinguished Opposition front-bencher, as he walked out past my Chair, said, 'Disgraceful, you're nothing but a Government stooge.' Another even more distinguished Opposition front-bencher as he went by said 'Brilliant'. It was an occasion for the Speaker to cultivate his selective deafness. My remark about a standing ovation, made at a time when the routine standing ovations at Party conferences were beginning to be regarded as boring and ridiculous, went well.

A very different incident took place a year later. In a way it was more difficult, but it only took a moment or so. On 31st January 1972, Maudling, then Home Secretary, made a statement about the tragic events in Londonderry on the previous day, during which a number of people had been killed.

Bernadette Devlin, then member for Mid-Ulster, interrupted the Minister to accuse him of lying. Later, during his answers to supplementary questions, she again accused him of lying. She then called him a murdering hypocrite.

The House was in a tense, emotional, excited mood. From the record, it could be said against me that at least three times I should have intervened to order Miss Devlin to withdraw her offending words. If she had failed to do so, I should have ordered her from the Chamber. If she had not gone, I should then have named her and the motion to suspend her would no doubt have been carried. She might then have had to be removed by force.

Again I thought it better to invoke my selective deafness, to take no notice of her allegations and to steer the House into quieter waters. I knew that the Opposition intended to apply later for an emergency debate under Standing Order No. 9, which I had decided to grant for the following day.

At some stage, Miss Devlin rose from her seat, ran across the floor of the House and physically assaulted Maudling.

There was uproar.

McManus, the member for Fermanagh and Tyrone,

came after her, apparently ready to engage in fisticuffs with anyone. In seconds it might have become a free for all. Mellish, the Opposition Chief Whip, and Murton, then a Government Whip, with commendable speed and presence of mind, hustled Miss Devlin out of the Chamber. Maudling sat there, calm and unruffled.

What was I to do?

There had been so much noise that, although I was on my feet, it was physically impossible for me to make myself heard until Miss Devlin was out of the Chamber. Therefore any action by me had to be after the event whether I liked it or not. I decided to take no action.

For this I was much criticized. The Leader of the House and the Government Chief Whip came to warn me of deep feeling on the Government side. I was told that it was by no means confined to Government supporters. The authority of the Chair and my personal position were in jeopardy. I must do something.

I took note of these warnings. Whitelaw and Francis Pym spoke not only in their official capacities but as close personal friends, and I decided to make a statement before the Irish debate.

I said,

I have considered what happened yesterday. When strong feelings exist or are aroused, there are times when the Chair can appropriately be deaf or indeed blind. In my view, I went to the absolute limits of tolerance, perhaps beyond them. What I now want to make clear is that if an hon. Member uses unparliamentary language or acts in an unparliamentary manner and when ordered to, refuses to withdraw or desist, I will not hesitate to act in accordance with the Standing Orders.

The reputation of the House and the position of the Chair are now at risk. That is something which I, so long as I am Speaker, cannot tolerate.

One or two members were not satisfied, and tried to pursue the matter with me. One obviously thought that I should have insisted on an apology from Miss Devlin. A motion of censure was put down, which according to my recollection attracted only three or four names. It was not debated.

I realized at the time that my action or lack of it would be criticized. But, in the prevailing atmosphere, no appeals from the Chair for withdrawal or apology would have had any effect. It would have ended in Miss Devlin being named and perhaps removed by force. She would at once have become a martyr. There might have been further riots in Northern Ireland, and the loss of more innocent lives.

There was another incident involving Bernadette Devlin. She was pregnant, and the baby was expected in a month or so. She came to the House to ask a question and I was told that she meant to make trouble for me and create a scene. After her question had been answered, she made some offensive remarks in her supplementary question. I took no notice, but when the Minister had replied I moved straight on to the next business, disregarding the dozen or so Labour Members who were on their feet also seeking to ask supplementaries.

Mellish came to me in the Chair afterwards and said that his Members were very upset. I had treated them badly. Would I receive a deputation? I replied that of course I would.

Some time later three senior Labour back-benchers came to see me to complain. I said that I thought that they had every right to do so. I had treated them unfairly and with scant courtesy. They ought to have had the chance to ask their questions, and in ordinary circumstances I would have called some of them. But would they answer me one simple question? How did I have a pregnant Member removed from the Chamber? If I named her, if her suspension was approved, and if she then refused to

withdraw, what did I do? Did I send for a policewoman
or an obstetrician or whom? What would be the result if
force was used and there was a miscarriage? Who was it
who would be called murderer?

The deputation withdrew in good order, having made a
perfectly fair point, but after our discussion perhaps with
more insight into the problems of the Chair.

The Chair came under similar criticism a few days later
on 10th February 1972. The miners' strike was taking
place. There was a Private Notice Question about the
distribution of fuel supplies in the Midlands. Strong feelings
had been aroused. Ministers were subjected to loud and
angry interruptions. I then called a lady Member for a
Midland constituency on the Opposition side to ask a
supplementary question. It was not a short one. In fact
it was the longest that I remember hearing from a back-
bencher, according to the Official Report 435 words in
all. I deliberately let her continue. At the beginning of her
question, the atmosphere was tense and trouble was brew-
ing, by the end both friends and foes were laughing. The
temperature had dropped perceptibly. There were points
of order and complaints from Government supporters, but
instead of the House working itself up into an attitude
which would have forced me to suspend the sitting, we
had covered difficult ground more easily than I expected.

The Speaker continually has to beware of taking action
against his better judgment for fear that he will otherwise
be thought weak.

In addition to 25th January 1971, I suspended the
sitting on several other occasions. On 20th January 1972,
when the unemployment figure had risen to one million,
the Opposition deliberately refused to allow the Prime
Minister to answer the first question put to him, and
shouted him down. I suspended the sitting for fifteen
minutes. On two other occasions it was suspended for
technical reasons, the time fixed for the next business not
having been reached. Once it was during an all-night

sitting to enable me to retire for a few minutes. On three occasions it was because the House was working itself up into a bad temper and a little time was needed to calm down or clear up a misunderstanding.

On 11th July 1974 there was a tie on two votes on Opposition amendments during the Report Stage of the Trade Union and Labour Relations Bill. Each time in accordance with precedent the Chair gave its casting vote against the amendment. The Bill then received its third reading and was sent up to the House of Lords. On 15th and 16th July it was raised as a point of order that Harold Lever, who owing to an illness found difficulty in walking, had been 'nodded' through the division lobby by the Whips, when absent from the House. The practice of 'nodding' a Member through is common when that Member is unwell or physically handicapped in some way, but the Member has to be on the premises at the time. Without Lever's vote there had not in fact been a tie, the Chair's casting vote would not have been given, and the amendments would have been carried. On 16th July the demand was made that a resolution should be passed asking for the Bill to be returned from the Lords, the amendments made, the Bill read again the third time, and sent up to the Lords in the form in which it would have been, but for Lever's vote having been wrongly counted. Ministers at first refused to agree to this, but Lever honourably rose and said that he had been absent, believing that it was not necessary for him to be there the whole time. Tempers began to rise and I suspended the sitting for twenty minutes. I told Ministers that in view of Lever's statement, I would have to say that the two votes were irregular and the record would have to be corrected, and that I expected the House to take the necessary action. This was eventually done. The suspension had served its purpose in calming down an excited House and giving time for back-bench opinion to make itself felt.

Later that month I suspended the sitting in rather

different circumstances. The Lords' amendments to the
Housing Bill were to be considered. The Lords had only
completed their consideration of the Bill that day. The
amendments were not available to all Members. As the
House tried to make progress, tempers began to rise, and
it was said on a point of order that for the House to agree
with amendments which it had not seen was making a
farce of parliamentary democracy. I suspended the sitting
for twenty minutes, during which time it became clear
that the amendments had not reached the Vote Office
until a few minutes before the discussion of them began.
The Leader of the House wisely adjourned the business
until the following day.

The parliamentary temperature is unpredictable. Out
of a clear sky there suddenly comes a storm. All seems
quiet, then a single interjection or incident produces
pandemonium. Speaker Denison described in his journal
such an occasion on 4th June 1863, 'The House was in a
touchy irritable mood: the slightest step on my part might
have raised a storm. It was a flare up all in a moment.
But such is always the case with the sharpest hurricane.
The barometer gives no notice.'

The barometer gives no notice. The Speaker, like Agag,
must walk delicately all the time. When the storm comes,
he can occasionally perform the role of a lightning con-
ductor, but he has to be wary.

When one is trying to lower the temperature in an
excited House, one has to be very careful. In 1971, when
Heath was Prime Minister, he was criticized at Question
Time by more than one Labour back-bencher for sailing
at week-ends, and so not being able to attend to affairs
of State. Wilson rather unwisely in my view joined in,
and thereby added to the uproar. I, having regard to
Wilson's addiction to golf, said, 'Order, it is time we got
back on to the fairway.' The House was amused, and
relaxed even more when Wilson prefaced the Business
Question a few moments later by saying, 'In view of your

comments, Mr. Speaker, as one whose drives never get on the fairway, but who whether on the fairway or in the rough was within five minutes of being able to resume his Prime Ministerial duties, unlike the Right Honourable Gentleman, I should like to ask ... ' I felt that I had drawn blood, but it only just worked.

In contentious debates, the main task is to see that Members get a fair hearing. This particularly applies to the final speeches on each side. Sometimes when a speaker was being deliberately provocative, I would think with sympathy of the remark of Sir Spencer Compton, Speaker from 1714 to 1722. A Member appealed to him to make the House quiet, declaring that he had a right to be heard. Compton replied, 'No, Sir, you have a right to speak, but the House has a right to judge whether it will hear you.'

In practice it is very much a matter of reciprocity. If one side has listened quietly, it is much easier for the Chair to persuade the other side to do the same. If one side noisily interrupts speakers from the other side, it must expect the same treatment for its own.

The events of Monday, 3rd March 1975, and Tuesday, 4th March, were typical of how a storm might suddenly arise, and as swiftly subside. Peace can break out as well as war.

The Report Stage of the Finance Bill was being taken on the Monday. There had been some preliminary skirmishing at the beginning, but the debate was continuing fairly quietly on various amendments. Then it became known that the Government were dissatisfied with the rate of progress and intended to put down a timetable motion, the guillotine.

Just after 11 p.m. there was a division. Joel Barnett, one of the Treasury Ministers, then moved that further consideration of the Bill be adjourned. The Opposition protested indignantly. They were prepared to sit all night if necessary to make progress. The Deputy in the Chair

(Murton) put the Question on the motion to adjourn and called, 'Clear the Lobby'. There was a stream of points of order as to whether or not he had collected the voices, whether he was right to have allowed the Leader of the House to say that he would make a statement after the division, and whether he should not let the debate continue. Murton eventually succeeded in putting the Question and there was a division.

I returned to the Chair during the division to find a seething House. I declared the result 269 to 257 a Government majority of 12.

I then called upon Edward Short, the Leader of the House. There were repeated attempts to get me to take points of order. I refused to do so until I had heard what Short had to say. He said in what he described as a short business statement that there would be a timetable motion relating to the Finance Bill to be taken as first business on the following day and also a motion on the Wednesday about financial assistance to the motor-cycle manufacturers Norton-Villiers Triumph Ltd.

Again there were attempts at points of order. I refused to take them until I had allowed John Peyton, the Shadow Leader of the House, to question Short. Peyton protested about the timetable motion, and asked why aid to Norton-Villiers had suddenly become so urgent. Short replied that it was because the chairman of the company had told the Government that if money were not forthcoming that week, there would be redundancies. I allowed Thorpe, the Liberal leader, to make a protest, and then said that contrary to precedent I would allow one point of order. In the extremely excited state of the House, I thought it prudent to give that much rope. I called Peter Emery, Conservative Member for Honiton. He queried whether the motion for the adjournment of consideration of the Bill had been properly put, and asked me to protect the rights of minorities. I replied that I always tried to protect the rights of minorities. The motion had been put; there had been a division. When Members shouted 'no' at me, I said that I thought that I had just announced the result. I had allowed the Leader of the House to make a statement, and allowed a supplementary question. That I said must be the end of it. The Opposition were furious with me and showed it in a full-throated manner. I said that they could shout at me as much as they liked, but I was going to call the motion for the adjournment of the House, which I did. There were attempts by John Gorst, Conservative Member for Hendon North, and Anthony Kershaw, Conservative Member for Stroud, to raise further points of order, but I refused to take them.

The first consequence was a motion of censure on me, which was tabled at once by Gorst.

I knew that the House would meet in an excited mood on the Tuesday, and decided to make a statement indicating the practice which I had established with regard to business statements not made at the usual time in the parliamentary day. I said that it had been to allow a statement by the Government spokesman and then one further question. I had called Short and then Peyton. I had refused points of order because in my view there could not possibly be a valid point of order. Short had used parliamentary language and the course which he had proposed was in accordance with Standing Orders. I commented on the abuse of using points of order to advance arguments. I said that if the House wanted a change of business to be announced some other way, the Procedure Committee might be asked to examine the matter. It might also consider how the Chair could be helped to deal with points of order.

That went quite well, but Emery challenged my right to stop a Member raising a point of order, and quoted Erskine May at me. I said that I had no desire to restrict Members raising points of order, but if the Chair thought that a point of order could not be a valid one, it must allow the House to get on with its business. Gorst said that he was satisfied with my statement and would withdraw his motion of censure. There was a rumble from Kershaw, but it subsided.

All had gone well so far.

Then Michael Heseltine, the Opposition spokesman on industry, raised as a point of order the fact that the Chairman of Norton-Villiers had told him that he had had no conversations with Ministers or Civil Servants that week. Wedgwood Benn replied instead of Short, but did not answer Heseltine's point. The Opposition became increasingly indignant and shouting, 'answer, answer', refused to allow the next business to begin. I suspended the sitting for twenty minutes. When we resumed, Short said that he had spoken the evening before in good faith. He had not intended to mislead the House. It had been during the previous week that the Chairman had spoken to Benn. He apologized. It was another example of a brief suspension giving Ministers time to reconsider their positions and tempers to cool. The House went fairly quietly on its way. The Government won its guillotine motion by a majority of nine.

## Debates

So much for the order and dignity of proceedings.

With certain minor exceptions, the Speaker has no control over the subjects for debate. They are settled by Government and Opposition, if not by agreement, certainly after discussion by what are called the 'usual channels', which means consultations between the Whips. There is by Standing Order a half-hour debate each day at the end of other business, on the motion for the adjournment of the House. It is then that private Members have the opportunity to raise matters involving the Government's administrative responsibilities. On four days of the week, the subject to be raised is chosen by ballot, but on one day the Speaker chooses it. He also chooses the subjects for discussion on the motion for the adjournment, which, after any questions and statements there may be, occupies the whole of the last day's sitting before each recess.

The Speaker selects the back-bench speakers from both sides of the House (again with one or two relatively minor exceptions).

When Speaker Shaw-Lefevre was in the Chair one day, more than twenty Members rose to catch his eye. A friend asked him how he contrived to single out his man. 'Well,' he is said to have replied, 'I have not been shooting rabbits all my life for nothing, and I have learnt to mark the right one.'

I did not find it easy. It was one of the most worrying, time-consuming and frustrating aspects of my work.

I often thought nostalgically of Colonel Henry Lowther and wished that there were more Members in our day like him. He was Speaker Lowther's grandfather and a Member from 1812 to 1867, when he died at the age of seventy-seven as Father of the House. He never once made a speech in all that time. He was a conscientious but silent Member.

The custom has grown up that Members who want to speak send in their names to the Speaker, usually with an accompanying letter giving special reasons. At one time, there used to be a list prepared by the Whips and given to the Speaker. I do not think that it happened during my time as a Member. It certainly did not while I was Speaker.

Some Members would cavil at the idea that they should write in beforehand. I used to explain that it was not at all obligatory, but that in important debates it was helpful to the Speaker. So often a balance had to be kept: each region ought to have its say; there were the Scots, the Welsh and the Northern Irish; there were industrial, county, urban, and suburban seats; there were the Privy Councillors. It was helpful to me to know beforehand at least most of those who wished to catch my eye.

I made what I think was a new rule with regard to Privy Councillors. The convention had been that Privy

Councillors should be called before other Members. It meant that in a foreign affairs debate, for example, the first two or three hours after the front-bench speeches might be taken up exclusively by Privy Councillors, all of them former Ministers or elder statesmen. This convention was bitterly resented.

I decided that I would not call two back-bench Privy Councillors of the same Party one after another. A non-Privy Councillor would be called in between. This change was, I think, welcomed by all except one or two of the Privy Councillors.

I believe that the number of Members wanting to speak in the big debates has grown steadily. I could never quite understand the fascination of the big debate for younger Members. Their audience would probably be confined to those also wanting to speak. They would be lucky to get even a mention in the national press, while their constituents would be much more interested to read that their Member had been haranguing the Commons about some local problem such as a projected road, rural buses, a new school or hospital or some other matter of local interest.

On the other hand, I felt great sympathy with those not called, going home with the notes of unmade speeches in their pockets, disconsolate and frustrated, and I used to get very angry with the selfish who made unreasonably long speeches.

There were times when the selection was complicated by minority views, not only the minority parties, but the minorities within the major parties. It was difficult to keep a fair balance in debates on Common Market affairs, defence, and some agricultural topics, for example the export of live cattle. In my last Parliament the existence of the Tribune and Manifesto groups within the Government ranks accentuated the problem. Nor could I ever persuade Members that I was not omniscient, that I really did not know beforehand their views on all topics, their quali-

The Speaker's Chair

The State Opening of Parliament, 1967. Black Rod summoning the Commons to hear the Queen's Speech in the Lords

The Speaker's procession on the terrace, (l. to r.) Doorkeeper, Serjeant at Arms, Mr Speaker, Trainbearer, Chaplain and Speaker's Secretary

The author with members attending a Commonwealth Parliamentary Association seminar inside Speaker's House

The author with (l. to r.) George Thomas (the present Speaker), Oscar Murton and Sir Myer Galpern

The author with Harold Wilson, Sir Alec Douglas-Home, Edward Heath and Emmanuel Shinwell at his ninetieth birthday party

The author with Nicolai Ceauşescu, President of the Socialist Republic of Rumania and General Secretary of the Rumanian Communist Party

The author with the Japanese Speaker opening the British Parliamentary Exhibition in Tokyo

The author welcoming Queen Juliana of the Netherlands to Speaker's House

fications, and the factories and numbers employed in each branch of industry in every constituency.

On my election in January 1971, I discovered that the system was for a list to be prepared of those who had written in, asking to be called, with a figure after each name showing how often that Member had spoken during the session. That gave me no idea of the topics on which the Member had spoken, nor did I know the dates and length of previous speeches. If a Member came to the Chair and asked to be called or rose without notice, I had no quick way of looking up the record.

Accordingly I started my Blue Book. When public reference was made to it on my retirement, there was difficulty in getting its colour right. It was called by Mrs Thatcher a Red Book, and by others a Black Book. In fact it had a bright blue cover. Every Member's name was in it. I kept it up to date myself, entering the date, subject and length of each back-bench speech. I did not record the speeches made on the daily adjournment motion, or those made during Committee or Report Stages. Friday was a day on which as a rule few Members tried to speak. I recorded a speech made on a Friday with an F after it, to show that it probably should not be counted against its maker. Before each big debate I would make a list of those wanting to speak, and fill in their records from the Blue Book, so that I and the Deputies would know the form.

I had a lot of fun with this book. Members would come to the Chair and I would say that I must look up their previous 'convictions'. A Member would say that he had only spoken once that session for seven minutes. I would look him up in the book and reply that on the contrary he had spoken four times, and never for less than fifteen minutes.

In the course of a debate the Speaker may be called upon to exercise two important discretions—to allow a motion to closure or a motion to adjourn a debate to be put. I have already described Speaker Brand's bold initiative in 1881, and subsequent developments. The present rule is that neither of these motions can be moved without the Speaker's permission or, since 1972, that of the Deputy in the Chair at the time. The phrase, 'the Speaker gives the closure', simply means that he gives the House the opportunity to vote upon it.

These discretions are not as a rule difficult to exercise. If the debate is a normal one, finishing at 10 p.m. from Mondays to Thursdays, or at 7 p.m. if it is a half-day debate, or one which has occupied the greater part of the day until 4 p.m. on a Private Members' Friday, the Speaker would almost certainly allow the closure motion to be put at those times. If it is during the Report Stage of a Bill, or on a motion dealing with the length of a recess, the Speaker would take into account whether the speeches made were obviously dilatory, the number of Members still wanting to speak, and whether minority views had been adequately expressed. One important safeguard against attempts at indiscriminate closuring is that under the Standing Order not less than one hundred Members must vote in the majority in support of a motion to closure a debate.

A motion to adjourn a debate to another day is rarely asked for without general agreement. Occasionally, however, the Opposition may claim that the Government have not given adequate answers to their questions, or that the debate has gone on too long for the House to continue it satisfactorily. The Opposition then try to persuade the Speaker to allow such a motion. It is not difficult to decide at the time whether there is good reason for it to be debated, or whether it is just a delaying tactic.

## Standing Order No. 9

An important discretion is given to the Speaker under Standing Order No. 9. From Monday to Thursday, a

Member can at the commencement of public business (in other words after questions, and any statements or rulings), move the adjournment of the House for the purpose of discussing a specific and important matter that should have urgent consideration.

The Speaker can then allow a debate upon it, either for three hours from the commencement of public business on the following day, or if he feels that the urgency of the matters requires it, from 7 p.m. until 10 p.m. on the same day.

This discretion I found difficult to exercise.

A Standing Order relating to emergency debates was first introduced in 1882. Its purpose was to curb the complete freedom which then existed for Members to move the adjournment of the House any day or several times a day to discuss particular matters. That freedom had become an easy means of obstructing the real business of the House.

To begin with, the Chair allowed many debates under the Standing Order. Between 1882 and 1920, 247 applications were allowed—an average of about 7 a year. Between 1921 and 1930, the number fell to 21. In the next thirty years, it was 19. Between 1961 and 1967, it was only 4. The reason for this was that the rulings of successive Speakers had restricted the interpretation of the words of the Standing Order to such an extent as to make it almost impossible for an application to succeed.

That was the situation which the Procedure Committee had to consider in 1967. I was then a member of the Committee and strongly in favour of some relaxation of the interpretation of the Standing Order, and of freeing the Chair from the mass of precedents for rejecting an application.

We recommended a change in the form of words from 'a definite matter of urgent public importance' to 'a specific and important matter that should have urgent consideration'. We also recommended that the decision should be within the Speaker's discretion. To make it easier for the

Speaker, and to prevent the accumulation of another load of precedents, we suggested that he should not give his reasons. We envisaged about five such debates a session.

Our report was approved by the House on 14th November 1967, and the Standing Order amended accordingly.

When I became Speaker, I began to realize some of the difficulties. The granting of an application inevitably disrupted the business already arranged. One of the sensible features in the way the House conducts its affairs is a fixed agenda, known beforehand. Each Thursday, the Leader of the House states the business for the following week. Members know where they are, when matters of particular interest to them are to be discussed, and when they should be in the Chamber. The disruption of the programme at short notice could be highly inconvenient.

There are always topics of general interest which should be debated. Either the Government ought to find the time, or the Opposition, with its considerable allowance of Supply Days, should do so. The Speaker's discretion under Standing Order No. 9 should not be used to enable the two main Parties to avoid finding time for such debates.

I allowed three in the 1970–71 Session. The first was when the Minister of Aviation and Supply announced that the Board of the Rolls-Royce Company had asked the trustees of the debenture holders to appoint a receiver and manager. He also stated that the Government were going to acquire certain of the assets of the company. The second time was in relation to an industrial dispute in the Post Office. The Government spokesman said that negotiations had broken down, that the executive of the Union had decided to continue the strike and that no action was intended by the Government. The third time was in relation to Upper Clyde Shipbuilders Ltd, when the Minister told the House of an application for a winding-up order.

In the 1971–2 session, I again allowed three applications under the Standing Order. The first was in relation to the

Compton Report about the behaviour of security forces in Northern Ireland. It was a very controversial statement of the position, which rapidly aroused strong feelings on both sides of the House. The second time again was with regard to Northern Ireland. The third time was when John Mendelson, a Labour Member, made an application for a debate about Vietnam. In all these cases there were deteriorating situations and it was quite obvious to me that there would be no chance of a debate unless I granted the application.

In the 1972–3 Session, I allowed one application relating to the hospital service. In the 1973–4 Session, I allowed one about the threat to coal supplies. In the 1974–5 Session, I allowed an application by Eric Ogden, a Labour Member, after the Government had announced the abandonment of the Channel Tunnel Project.

This total of nine in five years was far smaller than I had hoped for or expected, but in fact on several occasions I did persuade the Government or the Opposition to give time for a topic to be discussed which a Member wanted to raise under Standing Order No. 9.

On two occasions at least during my time, I was prepared to allow an application but none was made.

In July 1975, when the state of the British motor-cycle industry was raised, I would have granted an application under Standing Order No. 9 (in spite of its effect on an already over-crowded programme) but for the fact that I had control of the subjects to be debated on the motion for the adjournment of the House before the summer recess. This was to be taken in a few days time, when I allowed two and a half hours for a debate on the motor-cycle industry.

Nevertheless I was disappointed that I was not able to allow more adjournment debates under the Standing Order.

A typical example of the difficulties with which I so often had to deal occurred in October 1975. A Conservative

west midlands Member made an application for an emergency debate under Standing Order No. 9 on the grounds
that the figure for those unemployed had passed the million
mark. On that day some very controversial Lords' amendments to the Industry Bill were to be debated. A timetable motion was to be moved, fixing midnight as the time
at which the debate must end; the remaining Government
motions and amendments would then have to be put
without discussion. On the following day, there was to be
a long-awaited and more than once postponed debate on
Welsh affairs.

It would have been wrong of me to disrupt this programme. Nor was Standing Order No. 9 intended to cover
a continuing problem such as unemployment.

I ruled,

> My decision must not be construed by anyone as
> implying that I do not realize the importance of the
> problem. As a Merseyside Member I know it full well.
> But it is a continuing problem, one which should
> certainly be debated in this House on repeated occas-
> ions, but not one for which Standing Order No. 9 was
> drafted or intended. I am afraid that my answer
> which is a procedural one and no more, must be
> 'No'.

My conclusion was that Standing Order No. 9 was
extremely important. It was right that the House of Commons should from time to time have the opportunity of
emergency debates, but the Speaker's decisions were not
nearly so easy to make as I had thought when serving on
the Procedure Committee.

## Questions

The time allotted for questions to be answered orally is
2.35 to 3.30 p.m. from Monday to Thursday. There is a

roster according to which Ministers in charge of departments take it in turn to answer. The questions must be
put down to the appropriate Minister not more than ten
sitting days or less than two clear days before that Minister's
turn to answer. There are different rules for questions
requiring written answers.

Questions must ask for information or action relating
to current Government responsibilities and must not have
already been answered, or refused an answer, during the
previous three months. The Speaker has the final decision
as to the admissibility of a particular question.

The Speaker chooses those Members whom he allows to
put supplementary questions to a Minister after his initial
answer. The convention is to allow the Member who has
put down the question to ask the first supplementary, but
this is not a binding rule upon the Chair. The Speaker has
to strike a balance between reaching a reasonable number
of questions in the time available and permitting reasonable probing of the Minister's position. I took the view
that the number of questions reached was less important
than a searching examination of a Minister's conduct.
Perhaps that was one of the advantages of having a Speaker
who had himself been a Minister. I knew which gave less
trouble to the Minister.

I was interested to see my opinion confirmed by Dick
Crossman. He wrote in his diary on 16th November 1965
to the effect that although he was first for questions, he
did not have to bother with much preparation, as Question
Time was having the sting taken out of it: in the attempt
to have fifty or sixty questions answered each day, supplementaries were being curtailed. Crossman added, 'This
increases the enormous advantage which the Minister
enjoys.' Later he wrote, 'Life is too easy for Ministers
in our Parliament. Take Question Time. Now that
Questions have been speeded up, the last anxiety has been
removed.'

Of course it was irritating when a Member put a very

long-winded supplementary question, containing several separate points. The practice of the Opposition front bench (whichever Party was in power) intervening more often than not, was also unfair to the back-benchers. But that was a matter for protest by the back-benchers themselves. I did my best to show my disapproval of lengthy supplementaries and lengthy answers, but I believe that in this matter it is for the Members of the House to discipline both themselves and their colleagues. If the Chair takes it upon itself to do this, it would be intervening all the time, often ineffectually. Thus its authority would decrease.

The Speaker also has power under the Standing Orders to allow what are called Private Notice Questions (I will refer to them from now on as P.N.Q.s), ones which in his opinion are of an urgent character and relate either to matters of public importance or to the arrangement of business.

The rule is that notice has to be given to the Speaker through his office by noon. As soon as a P.N.Q. has been notified, the Table Office is informed and in turn seeks information about its subject-matter from the appropriate Department. This is a necessary step, and helpful to the Speaker. For example, on one occasion when a leading member of the Opposition wanted to ask the Foreign Secretary about a conference which he had been attending, I learnt from the Department that the aircraft in which the Foreign Secretary was returning, would not land until 4 p.m. and he intended anyhow to make a statement on the following day.

On occasions Ministers tried to make direct representations to me or send messages through my Secretary, asking me not to allow a particular question. I had to insist that any attempt to put pressure on me personally would be counter-productive, and that any such representation must be made through the Table Office. In time that came to be accepted by Ministers of both Parties.

In a normal week of five days (because P.N.Q.s could be allowed on a Friday), application would be made for perhaps fifteen, several probably on the same subject. One had, therefore, to work out certain guide lines, helped of course by the practice of previous Speakers.

The convention is that a P.N.Q. from the Leader of the Opposition is always accepted. That right was rarely claimed in my time and never abused. If the Shadow Foreign Secretary, Chancellor of the Exchequer or Home Secretary put down a P.N.Q., it was difficult to refuse it. If I felt that I had to refuse it, without an obvious reason, I would explain my reasons to the Opposition Chief Whip for him to pass on. It might be that I knew that the Minister concerned intended to make a statement on the matter in the next day or two. It might be that I was firmly of the opinion that it would not be in the national interest to have the question put and answered, with other Members who possessed less knowledge or sense of responsibility joining in. It might be that the pressure of other business in the House that day was very great—statements, rulings, a Ten Minute Rule Bill, a half-day debate on an Opposition motion, or a long-awaited full-day debate with fifty or sixty Members wanting to speak. If the P.N.Q. was about an industrial dispute, I might refuse it because I knew that an important meeting was taking place that day, and that ventilation of the dispute in the House of Commons might make the settlement more difficult.

Whatever guide lines one tried to establish, the exercise of this discretion required much care and thought. It was impossible to be entirely logical and consistent. It was a case of exercising one's judgment as best one could from day to day. As usual the Speaker has to strike a balance. On the one hand the House of Commons should be seen to be examining Ministers on matters of topical interest. It should not be left to the television interviewer; his turn can come later. On the other hand, no one can guarantee that nothing will be said in the House to make a difficult situation worse. In addition each P.N.Q. with the answer and supplementaries takes fifteen minutes or more. If it has been put down not to obtain information but merely to continue a political argument, the time of the House must be protected.

A classic example, in my opinion, of how the P.N.Q. system should be used occurred towards the end of 1973. The Opposition front-bench spokesman asked to put a P.N.Q. to the Home Secretary about the imminent deportation of seven Chileans. They had come to this country from France and wished to stay until places could be found for them at universities. The House was about to rise for the Christmas recess, returning on 15th January 1974. I asked the Table Office to find out from the Department whether the Chileans were to be deported before the House reassembled. I said that if I received an undertaking that it would not happen before the House reassembled, I would not allow the P.N.Q. The Home Office could not give that assurance. Accordingly I allowed the P.N.Q. I describe this as a classic case for allowing a P.N.Q. because action might have been taken by a Minister about which he could not be questioned in the normal way until after it had happened.

It is an important convention that if a P.N.Q. is refused, the Speaker should not be asked in the House for his reasons nor indeed should the application be mentioned. This is because the Speaker cannot be expected each time to justify his reasons for refusing a P.N.Q. It would take up far too much parliamentary time. Unless he can defend or explain his decision, the raising of the matter is obviously undesirable. On the whole this convention has been honoured.

Difficult cases to decide were those relating to fatalities, whether accidental or by design. If, for example, the Speaker allowed a P.N.Q. about every road accident, there would be a number each day. On 1st December 1975 I tried to give the House an explanation of the guide lines which, in the light of experience, I had adopted

It is in general only to allow Private Notice Questions relating to fatalities first if the incident is of disaster proportions; secondly if the incident appears to represent some totally new development; and, thirdly, if it seems that urgent action of a particular kind might be suggested, to prevent other people suffering a similar fate. I try to exercise my discretion along these lines in each case as it arises.

On reflection I think the word 'totally' in relation to new development went too far. Having that consideration in mind, I allowed a P.N.Q. about the murder of Ross McWhirter. Someone then reminded me that over fifty years before, Field-Marshal Sir Henry Wilson had been killed in the same way.

## Personal Statements

Another important matter which lay within the Speaker's discretion was the making by a Member of a personal explanation or personal statement. It is stated in Erskine May, 'In regard to the explanation of personal matters, the House is usually indulgent; and will permit a statement of that character to be made without any question being before the House provided that the Speaker has been informed of what the Member proposes to say and has given leave.'

The Speaker's task could be very simple. If a Member wished to correct an inaccuracy in something that he had said or was reported to have said, leave would always be given, provided there were no complications. But there were times when the decision was not easy.

On 11th June 1975 I allowed Judith Hart to explain the reasons why she had left the Government, but I did not ask to see the contents of the statement beforehand. The following day a point of order was raised as to the propriety of what had happened, on the ground that her statement had contained reflections upon other Members.

In reply I affirmed the practice that the permission of the Chair should in all cases be sought. It had been by Mrs Hart, and I had given it. I stated, however, that when it was an explanation by a Member of the circumstances under which he or she had resigned it was not necessary for the Speaker to approve the statement. I said that that would be putting too great a burden upon the Chair. The contents of such a personal statement must be a matter for the judgment of the Member concerned.

I added that in other cases not only should the permission of the Chair be sought but the terms of the statement should be approved by the Chair.

In October 1975, John Stonehouse had returned to this country from Australia and sought leave to make a personal statement to the House. The advice which I received was that I had complete discretion as to the contents of a personal statement submitted to me, but it should be un-controversial and not likely to give rise to debate. All the instances in Erskine May related only to words or actions in the House.

I found the word 'uncontroversial' difficult. It could be said that every explanation, even of a simple mistake, could be controversial. Why had the mistake been made? Was the Member culpable or not? I thought that the words likely to give rise to debate were a sounder guide. 'Words or actions in the House' could clearly include Stonehouse's case. After much thought and discussion with my advisers, and after a lengthy interview with Stonehouse himself, followed by discussions between him and the Clerks, I passed a statement for him to make. The most important factor in my mind was that his absence and conduct had been referred to frequently in the House. A Select Committee had been set up in January 1975 after nearly three hours of debate, and a division, to consider his position. The Select Committee had reported to the House. It was only fair to allow him to make a statement. Having said this to the House before the statement was made, I added, 'As to the precise contents of the statement the task of the Chair in this case has been to ensure that nothing should be said in it concerning matters which are sub judice, and that it does not involve attacks upon other Members.'

I felt that I could not pretend that the statement would be uncontroversial. On the other hand, as passed by me, I did not think that it would be likely to give rise to a debate, in view of the criminal proceedings by then under way.

I ended by saying that the convention of the House was that a personal statement should be listened to in silence. The House certainly rose to the occasion, if that is the right phrase to use. The Right Honourable Member was listened to in complete silence, except that I had to pull him up several times for departing from the text which I had passed.

If he had not been allowed to make a statement, I believe that there would have been a widespread feeling that he had not had fair treatment.

The conclusion which I think should be drawn from these cases is that precedents or guide lines should exist, but that the Speaker must look at each case on its merits, and exercise his discretion without feeling himself too tightly bound by previous rulings.

## Casting Vote

If there is a tie, the Speaker must give a casting vote. He cannot adopt the Swedish practice under which, when the votes are equal, the Talsmand of the Riksdag has to draw lots. In November 1974, Mr Allard, then Talsmand, told a friend of mine that in a House where the Government and Opposition Parties were equally balanced with 175 seats each, only 18 out of 400 divisions had been tied. He claimed jocularly that his impartiality had been proved to be not less than that of the British Speaker: on 9 occasions out of these 18 the lot had been drawn for the Government and on 9 against them.

The principles upon which the Speaker acts are now well recognized by the House. In the event of a tie he casts his vote for further discussion, or, if no further discussion is possible, against a final decision for change.

The First Reading of a Bill is a formality, but the Second Reading usually involves a wide-ranging debate. If there were to be a tie in the division on the Second Reading, the Speaker would vote 'aye' to allow opportunity for further discussion.

After a Bill has received a Second Reading, it goes to a committee, either a Standing Committee upstairs, or a Committee of the whole House. Then it comes back again to the House for the Report Stage. If there is a tie on an amendment moved during that stage, the Speaker votes for the Bill as it left the committee and against the amendment, whether it is moved on behalf of the Government or of the Opposition.

If there were to be a tie on the Third Reading, the final stage, the Speaker would vote 'no' on the grounds that a change in the law requires a majority in the House, and should not be made on the Speaker's casting vote. The same would apply to a motion whether moved by the Government or not.

I have already mentioned the occasion in July 1974 when a tie was announced by the tellers, which afterwards proved not to have been a tie in fact. I will return later to it when dealing with the general election of October 1974.

## Selection of Amendments

Perhaps the most important of the discretions entrusted to the Speaker is the power to select the amendments to be discussed. In the case of motions, or Bills at their Second Reading, Report Stage or Third Reading, the Speaker has complete discretion.

A similar power is given to the Chairman of a Standing Committee, or if a Bill is in Committee of the whole House, to the Chairman of Ways and Means.

Speaker Lowther objected to this discretion being given to the Chair, because he thought that it imposed too onerous a burden. But he lived in different days. At present, unless the Speaker had this power of selection, there would have to be a timetable motion for the Report Stage of most Bills.

I think that I went rather further than my predecessors in encouraging informal discussions between the Clerk who had functioned during the Committee Stage and the Opposition spokesmen, before I made my selection. After discussing with the Clerk the amendments or new clauses tabled, and the length of the debates which would arise, I would try to find out the Opposition's priorities, in other words the degree of importance which they attached to each. The Clerk would have informal discussions with the Opposition spokesmen, or, if a private Member had put down a lot of amendments, he would be asked for his priorities, and I would probably select accordingly. This system worked quite well. The selected list was posted in the Lobby marked 'provisional'. That left scope for reconsideration as the business proceeded.

Throughout my time as Speaker, I felt some sympathy with the smaller minority Parties. It was quite right that, with the two major Parties having 600 or so Members out of 635, the issues voted upon should be those chosen by them. If, for example, there was an official Opposition amendment to a Government motion on an important topic, and there were also amendments from the smaller Parties, I could say that the amendments could all be discussed together. Usually, however, it was procedurally impossible to have a vote on one of the smaller Party's amendments after the official Opposition's, because the debate had, under Standing Orders, to end at 10 p.m. There would then be a vote. After that, it being about

10.15, it was procedurally impossible for another amendment to be moved and voted upon.

I put this matter to the Select Committee on Procedure and they accepted my suggestion that the Government should put down a business motion allowing another amendment to be formally moved after the main Opposition one had been decided upon. This was done at the end of the debate upon the Address, in November 1975, and also at the end of a four-day debate on devolution in January 1976. I refused to suggest it for the one-day debate about unemployment that same month on two grounds. First, it would have been going far beyond the Committee's recommendation. Second, if it was allowed on unemployment, why not every time there was a major one-day debate? So wide an innovation should only be introduced on the authority of the House itself.

## Divisions Unnecessarily Claimed

To prevent obstruction, the Speaker has a power under Standing Order No. 36, which is rarely used. A division can take up to fifteen minutes, and if a small group of Members persists in demanding divisions, that can amount to obstruction.

The Speaker puts the Question (for example, 'That the amendment be made'), then after a lapse of two minutes, he says, 'Ayes to the right, noes to the left' and announces the tellers (two for each side). Under Standing Order No. 36 he can, if he thinks the division is unnecessarily claimed, and before naming the tellers, take the vote of the House by calling upon the Members who support his decision and those who challenge it to rise successively in their places. He can then either declare the determination of the House, or name the tellers and allow the division to proceed.

I used this power on only one occasion. In July 1975 the House was taking the Report Stage of the Industry

Bill. The timetable motion had laid down that the guillotine should fall at 11 p.m. Discussion of the amendments then had to cease, and all outstanding Government amendments had to be moved formally, but they could of course be divided upon.

There was a vote at 11 p.m. on an Opposition amendment. The Government won by 222 to 209. Then the next Government amendment was moved. It was carried by 222 votes to 13. Then a Liberal Member gave notice that he requested a division on every one of the twenty or so Government amendments outstanding. After I had remonstrated, he reduced the number to six amendments on which he would claim divisions. The figures in the division on the next one were 222 to 15. After the next amendment had been approved without a division, a division was claimed on the following one. I invoked Standing Order No. 36. As only 13 Members challenged my decision, I declared the amendment carried.

Then I had a series of points of order. What was the criterion upon which I acted? Was it qualitative or quantitative? If my discretion was determined merely by numbers, was it not the doom of every minority in the House? I replied that I considered that I had to decide whether a division was purposeless and whether we were wasting time. It was then put to me by a Liberal Member, a lawyer, that I could judge purposelessness only by having regard to numbers. I replied, 'One of the troubles of my position is that I am invested with great discretions, which I must administer as best I can, I think seldom to the satisfaction of everybody. This is a case in which I am exercising my discretion. I feel that we must get on.'

The Liberals then agreed to ask for only two more divisions, and I allowed them in the usual form. The Government won by 199 to 14 on the first and by 208 to 13 on the second.

If there had been divisions on all twenty amendments, it would probably have taken four or five hours; as it was,

4

we managed it, including the points of order and divisions, in about fifty minutes. The Standing Order had proved its worth.

## Privilege

I now come to privilege and contempt of the House. The Speaker's task is to rule whether a motion relating to an alleged breach of privilege or contempt of the House should be given priority over other business. The modern custom is for him to take twenty-four hours to consider the matter. If the Speaker decides in the affirmative, a motion is usually moved that the matter be referred to the Committee of Privileges, a Select Committee of the House. But sometimes the matter is disposed of there and then by the House.

What the privileges of Members are and what constitutes contempt of the House opens up an abstruse and complicated subject.

In early days the Commons had to fight tenaciously for its privileges not only against the Crown, but also against the House of Lords. The privileges claimed by the Speaker-Elect at the beginning of each Parliament are 'freedom of speech in debate', 'freedom from arrest' and 'free access to Her Majesty'. With regard to contempt, Erskine May's definition is as follows

> It may be stated generally that any act or omission which obstructs or impedes either House of Parliament in the performance of its functions, or which obstructs or impedes any member or officer of such House in the discharge of his duty or which has a tendency directly or indirectly to produce such results may be treated as a contempt even though there is no precedent of the offence.

The High Court of Parliament and other Courts have

not always seen eye to eye on these matters, although a continuing open conflict has been avoided.

The present tendency is for the Commons not to seek to extend the area of privilege or contempt. I am sure that this is right.

As Leader of the House in 1964, I was Chairman of the Committee of Privileges when a complaint was made against Quintin Hogg, then Lord President of the Council. He had said in a speech, 'No honest person since we came to power can accuse us of pursuing a reactionary, or illiberal policy. Nevertheless our elbows have been jarred in almost every part of the world by individual Labour members' partisanship of subversive activities.'

This was referred to the Committee of Privileges. This is in many ways the senior committee of the House, with its members chosen from those with most experience. A well-known parliamentary journalist referred to it recently as 'a collection of bores, windbags, proven incompetents, ministerial rejects and political derelicts'. That judgment is a matter of opinion.

The committee over which I presided consisted of Birch, George Brown, Chuter Ede, Grimond, Geoffrey Lloyd, Mitchison, Nugent, Pickthorn, Turton and Harold Wilson.

We stated in our report what has always been my own attitude,

> Your Committee recognise that it is the duty of the House to deal with such reflections upon Members as tend, or may tend, to undermine public respect for and confidence in the House itself as an institution. But they think that when the effect of particular imputations is under consideration, regard must be had to the importance of preserving freedom of speech in matters of political controversy and also, in case of ambiguity, to the intention of the speaker. It seems to them particularly important that the law of parliamentary privilege should not, except in the clearest

case, be invoked so as to inhibit or discourage the formation and free expression of opinion outside the House by Members equally with other citizens in relation to the conduct of the affairs of the nation.

It has long been accepted that neither House of Parliament has any power to create new privileges. Your Committee believe that it would be contrary to the interest of the House and of the public to widen the interpretation of its privileges especially in matters affecting freedom of speech. Your Committee and the House are not concerned with setting standards for political controversy or for the propriety, accuracy or taste of speeches made on public platforms outside Parliament. They are concerned only with the protection of the reputation, the character and the good name of the House itself. It is in that respect only and for that limited purpose that they are concerned with imputations against the conduct of individual Members.

The Commons should not seek to extend the areas of privilege or contempt.

During my time as Speaker I had a variety of cases on which to rule. I rejected the formula 'a prima facie case' because I thought that it implied my belief that there was substance in the complaint. I contented myself with ruling whether or not I would give a motion relating to the particular matter precedence over the business of the day.

The cases put to me differed very much. The first, soon after I became Speaker, was a complaint about an assault upon a servant of the House. The incident took place on 28th January 1971, after a division had been called. I have already described how the Speaker puts the Question, waits for two minutes, puts it again and then names the tellers. Members meanwhile are gathering in the division lobbies. Under the Standing Order at least four more minutes must be allowed before the occupant of the Chair calls out, 'Lock the doors.' The Doorkeepers then close the doors to the Lobbies and no more Members can enter them to vote.

It was alleged that on the day in question, after the order to lock the doors had been given, some Members rushed into one of the lobbies pushing the Doorkeeper out of the way and preventing him from locking the doors until they were in the lobby. This was so clearly a case of alleged obstruction of a servant of the House in the discharge of his duty that I did not wait until the next sitting-day to rule. I gave a motion relating to it precedence, which was approved.

The Clerk of the House in his evidence to the Committee of Privileges quoted another passage in Erskine May, 'to prevent, delay, obstruct or interfere with the execution of the orders of either House or of Committees of either House is a contempt.' The Committee found that what had happened could well be a contempt, but they recommended that as there had been no deliberate assault upon the Doorkeeper, and no intention to prevent him from carrying out his duties, no further action should be taken by the House. The matter was not pursued. I agreed with the conclusion that no further action should be taken, and that no deliberate assault had been intended, but I did not understand the finding of fact that there had been no intention to prevent the Doorkeeper from carrying out his duties, namely, to lock the door. However, the report was not contested.

Other cases in my time raised issues of considerable importance. On 7th March 1972, the Committee reported on a case in which a newspaper published an article purporting to give an account of proceedings in a Select Committee not yet reported to the House. A resolution of the House passed in 1837 forbade this. The Committee found the journalist concerned guilty of a contempt, but it added some wise words, 'The Principal offender is the person who provided Mr. —— with the information. The person who provided that information committed a deliberate and flagrant contempt of the House.' The journalist's apologies were accepted.

On 25th November 1975, the Committee reported on a similar case in which a weekly newspaper published an article giving details of a draft report circulated to a Select Committee for consideration at its next meeting. The Committee stated that it considered the principal offender to be the person who provided the information, but also proceeded to state that if they had had the power, they would have fined the newspaper concerned, and they recommended that the editor and the journalist concerned should be excluded from the precincts of the House for six months.

I had my doubts about the wisdom of this recommendation. It produced cries in the Press that Parliament was making a collective ass of itself and that the public, through the media, had the right to know everything that was going on. I agree that they should know almost everything, but it is a matter of timing. Some confidential information and confidences should be kept confidential, certainly for a time. Frequently it is a matter of taste how long that time should be. But if journalists can find something out, it should be printed. The fault lies with the person who gives the information, particularly as in this case it was apparently not given to the journalist on a confidential basis but for publication.

The report was not accepted by the House, and an amendment was approved by 66 votes to 57 (including the tellers) in the terms that the House 'while regretting the leakage of information from the Select Committee on a Wealth Tax and its publication by *The Economist*, considers that no further action need be taken'.

It was, as is usual with such reports, a free vote. In other words, the Party Whips were not on. The speeches were interesting, and the voting not at all on Party lines.

Another case concerned the alleged serving of a writ

upon a Member in the precincts of the House. It is a contempt to serve or attempt to serve a civil or criminal process within the precincts, while the House is sitting, without obtaining its leave. In this case there was some doubt about whether the writ had technically been served, and the Committee accepted the assurance of the solicitors concerned that they had not intended directly or indirectly to impede the Member in pursuing what he believed to be his parliamentary duty. They found that no contempt had been committed.

On 29th April 1974, it was complained that a Member had alleged in an article and a radio interview that a number of Members had, for money, surrendered to outside bodies their freedom of action as Parliamentarians. The Committee were of the opinion that the conduct alleged would itself amount to a most grave contempt of the House. They considered that a Member should not make such an allegation about his fellow Members otherwise than in the course of proceedings in Parliament and for the purpose of drawing the attention of the House to those Members' conduct. They reached the conclusion that the Member's behaviour in making the allegation outside the House and without identifying the Members, was conduct likely to bring the House and its Members into disrepute, and accordingly constituted a serious contempt. They accepted, however, the Member's apology.

In July 1971, a complaint was made about a passage in a newspaper stating that 'a union yesterday threatened to withdraw cash support from pro-Market M.Ps. if they divided the Party. They were told to toe the line ... or join the Tories'. This complaint had been made before in other cases with negative results. In this instance the union official responsible denied any threat to withdraw financial support from M.Ps., and his denial was accepted.

The Committee's report quoted a passage in a previous report, approved by the House on 15th July 1947, 'It is a breach of privilege to take or threaten action which is not merely calculated to affect the Member's course of action in Parliament but is of a kind against which it is absolutely necessary that Members should be protected if they are to discharge their duties as such independently and without fear of punishment or hope of reward.'

In one case I rather reluctantly came to the conclusion that I could not give a motion precedence. It was when the supply of House of Commons' documents to Members was being delayed by industrial action. Such action certainly came within Erskine May's formula of impeding a Member in the discharge of his duty. However, the view had always been taken, no doubt for pragmatic reasons, that the Speaker should not seek to bring such action within the sphere of privilege or contempt. I complied, but with considerable hesitation, on the ground that I did not think that the limits of privilege or contempt should be extended.

## Sub Judice

Another of the Speaker's important discretions is with regard to matters sub judice. Erskine May states the rule in simple terms, 'matters awaiting the adjudication of a Court of Law should not be brought forward in debate'. It is not in fact as simple as that. Although the rule was seldom invoked in my time, I had to be able to decide at short notice whether to stop discussion or not.

The House had passed a resolution on the matter on 23rd July 1963. Its effect was that, subject to the discretion of the Chair and the right of the House to legislate upon any matter, issues awaiting or under adjudication in criminal courts, courts martial, and tribunals under the Tribunals of Enquiry (Evidence) Act 1921, should not be referred to in the House. In civil cases the rule was that until the case had been set down for trial or otherwise brought before the Court, as for example by notice of motion for an injunction, it could be referred to in the House unless the Speaker thought that there was real danger of prejudice to the trial of the case.

I put my own view to the Procedure Committee of 1971–2, when it considered the matter, in fairly simply terms. It was right that the discretion should remain with the Chair, but in criminal cases, etc. the onus should be upon those who sought to disregard the rule. In civil cases, other than defamation, the onus should be upon those who sought to invoke the rule.

Broadly speaking that view was accepted by the Committee, in their report in June 1972. They agreed that the 1963 Resolution should still apply to criminal cases, courts martial and Tribunals of Enquiry, and to proceedings for defamation in civil courts. All other matters before a civil court could be referred to unless there was real and substantial prejudice to the proceedings.

I remember, in particular, four cases in which I had to construe the sub judice rule. The first was the thalidomide case, that of the children on whose behalf proceedings had been begun against the Distillers Company, who had been responsible for marketing the drug which had caused such serious physical damage. The cases had not been set down for trial or otherwise brought before the Court. I had no hesitation in allowing debate. The Master of the Rolls, Lord Denning, in a judgment discharging an injunction upon the *Sunday Times* restraining it from publishing an article upon this tragedy, made these comments. He quoted the Bill of Rights, 'the freedom of speech and debate or proceedings in Parliament ought not to be impeached or questioned in any court or place out of Parliament', and he added that Parliament had the exclusive right to regulate its own proceedings. He went on to point out the wisdom of the sub judice rules being the same for Parliament and the Courts. He accepted that the reason for Parliament having discussed the matter was no doubt that the cases had not been set down for trial. He did not think that the trial would be prejudiced and he added, 'If their Lordships in their Court applied rules as to sub judice on the same lines as Parliament they would not go far wrong.'

In another series of cases arising out of the Industrial Relations Act 1971, I did seek to take matters a little further. Members feared that I would prevent discussion in the House of industrial matters, because some case had been brought in the Industrial Court. I invoked the sub judice rule very sparingly. I did not think that the fact that there were proceedings pending should prevent the discussion of national issues in the House. For example, the fact that a firm in the north west had referred a dispute about the manning or filling of containers to the Industrial Court, should not prevent all issues affecting containers from being discussed in the House.

The third case concerned what were called 'the Shrewsbury Pickets'. In November 1974 both Opposition and Government Members sought to raise the question of a free pardon for the convicted men. I ruled them out of order, thereby attracting considerable dissent from both sides of the House. The two men had appealed, and in my view any discussion in the House about the granting of a pardon might well prejudice their appeals. It would be unfair to them because it implied that the House accepted their guilt, although it had not been finally established in the courts.

The fourth case concerned the Crossman diaries. In 1975 the Attorney-General had applied for an injunction against their publication. I did not allow questions, as the case had been set down on the same day for hearing in four weeks time.

On 18th July, a Friday, a petition was presented by the Solicitor-General on behalf of the Attorney-General asking for leave to be given to the proper officers of the House to give evidence in Court, proving certain reports of debates in the House. No notice of the petition was needed or given, but both sides of the House took exception. It was thought that the Government were guilty of sharp practice in trying to push their motion through without notice on a Friday when the House would be empty. The debate lasted nearly an hour and was then adjourned. It was continued for two hours from midnight on 21st July, but no decision was reached as fewer than forty Members remained to vote. There was a substantial element of leg-pulling in all this, but the curious point did arise that the leave of the House is needed before an officer can give evidence in a Court authenticating the Official Record. A resolution in 1818 laid this down when the House was rather more touchy about the reporting of its proceedings. In my opinion, if any such restriction is needed, the practice whereby the Speaker can give leave in a recess should be extended to when the House is sitting.

## Minorities

Finally, but high in importance, is the Speaker's duty towards minorities. For obvious reasons the big Parties do not care for minority Parties. Equally the big Party establishments do not care for minorities within their own ranks. Frequently Members of the big Parties would come up to me in the Chair and respectfully suggest that Members of the big Parties also had their rights. I have already mentioned the procedural innovations which I sought to encourage (page 96). At Question Time and in debates, I took a great deal of trouble to try to be fair.

To show that to some extent I succeeded, but also to show the importance attached by minority Parties to them, I quote from the speeches made when I retired.

MR JEREMY THORPE: You have sought to see that in our debates all shades of opinion were fairly represented. Minorities within parties have always existed, and this has been something that all Speakers have come to accept. But in a situation, now, in which there are more parties than there have been in 50 years, you have suggested that perhaps our procedures have not caught up as quickly as you would have wished. But it has been your task to see that, with the fairness with which you have held the ring, all shades of opinion have fairly been recognised. The scrupulous fairness is something for which I, as a member of a minority party, feel deeply grateful.

MR J. ENOCH POWELL: It is a privilege which may fittingly be claimed by members of minorities and even small minorities in this House to join in the tribute to that servant of the House whose especial care is for the rights of individual Members and for the rights of minorities, however small. We know how faithfully you have discharged that part of your duty.

Donald Stewart for the S.N.P. and Gwynfor Evans for Plaid Cymru spoke in generous terms to the same effect.

The Speaker is in fact the only effective protector of the rights of minorities. This is immensely important. If these rights are not protected, a heavy and perhaps insupportable strain would be put upon our democratic machinery.

## IV

# Daily Routine and Personal Arrangements

Dame Irene Ward, when proposing me for election in 1971, said 'I wonder whether we could not find some way of reducing the isolation of the Speaker. The Speaker can be very lonely: he can be much away from the friendship and the affection of his parliamentary colleagues, which he has previously enjoyed.'

In seconding me, Pannell said that he hoped that I would not be as remote as previous Speakers had been.

Harold Wilson pursued the same theme in his speech oi congratulations,

In expressing our personal good wishes to you in the lonely task which you are taking up, and in expressing to you also the view that if you can find some ways of breaking that loneliness and even removing the convention of remoteness, you will have many right honourable and honourable gentlemen on both sides who will be willing to help you to do it.

These well-meant expressions of concern reflected certain misconceptions, even on the part of very experienced Members, about the Speaker's daily life while the House is sitting.

Members of the general public often used to express

to me a similar concern about my life as Speaker. They
seemed to think that I spent almost all my time in the
Chair either listening to boring speeches or trying to keep
order in a permanently disorderly House. When not doing
either of these things, I apparently sat in solitude in Speaker's
House.

The reality was very different. I have already dealt
with the subject of keeping order in the Chamber. I
admit that when I was elected I found that the time
I had to spend in the Chair or be available to return
to it at short notice was excessive. There were three
reasons.

First, on the face of it a technical matter, a considerable
amount of parliamentary time is devoted to what is called
the business of Supply. On those days, the Opposition
chooses the subject for debate. It is one of the most important features in our system, and means that the Government of the day has only a limited control over the agenda.
Time must be found for the Opposition to raise topics
which it wants to have debated. In December 1966, the
House accepted a report of the Procedure Committee that
the Committee of Supply should be abolished and the
number of days devoted to Supply should be twenty-nine
in each session. The effect upon the Speaker was considerable. From then on he had to be in the Chair on
Supply days. Before this change, when Supply was taken in
Committee of the whole House, the Deputy Speaker in his
capacity as Chairman of Ways and Means took the Chair,
(sitting in what is called the Lower Chair on the right
below the Speaker's Chair), relieved from time to time by
the Deputy Chairman of Ways and Means and any of the
members of the panel of chairmen, nominated at the
beginning of each session by the Speaker. This panel
consists of at least ten experienced Members who act as
chairmen of Standing Committees, and are also entitled
to sit as chairman of a Committee of the whole House.
For a Committee of the whole House there is accordingly

an abundance of Members qualified to occupy the Chair. Until the change in December 1966, the Speaker was relieved of duty in the Chair from the time the debate on the chosen subject began, usually about 4 p.m., until at least 10 p.m. Also the task of selecting the speakers fell upon the Deputy Speaker. The Procedure Committee realized the substantial extra burden which would be laid upon the Speaker by the change, and recommended that a second Deputy Chairman of Ways and Means should be appointed. This recommendation had not been implemented when I became Speaker.

Secondly, except when the business of Supply was being taken or during the Report Stage of a Bill, only the Speaker could allow a motion for the closure of a debate to be put. That meant that he had to be available to return to the Chair whenever the request for such a motion was likely to be made and often at short notice. Also he could never leave the Palace of Westminster until after 4 p.m. on a Friday, without a formal announcement that he would not be available. If such an announcement was made, the Deputy Speaker assumed the Speaker's powers.

Thirdly, that the Speaker had only two deputies who could relieve him meant that he himself had to be available to share late duty every night. As one of the deputies almost always did the last period, the Speaker could not keep them both on duty every night. In the twenty-one sitting days excluding Fridays after 18th January 1971, the House sat until after 11.30 p.m. on twenty of them and after 2 a.m. on nine of them.

After the strains and stresses of the first session of the 1970 Parliament, I managed to persuade the Government and Opposition to agree to the appointment of a Second Deputy Chairman of Ways and Means. In November 1971 the Standing Orders were amended to provide for this and Lance Mallalieu, Labour Member for Brigg, was appointed. It was also agreed that the Deputy who was in the Chair should have all the Speaker's powers (with one small exception). This made a vast difference. I myself rarely had to be in the Chair after 10.30 p.m. Nor did I have to be available at all hours on an ordinary sitting day or until 4 p.m. on a Friday to allow a closure motion to be moved. With a constituency over two hundred miles from London, I had found this latter obligation a considerable inconvenience.

During the Parliament from March to October 1974, a second Deputy was not appointed. There was not much legislation, sittings were not very late on most days, and the burden was just tolerable for the not very many weeks involved. However, I renewed my representations after the October general election and in October 1974, in addition to George Thomas as Deputy Speaker and Oscar Murton as Deputy Chairman of Ways and Means, Sir Myer Galpern, Labour Member for Shettleston, was appointed Second Deputy Chairman of Ways and Means.

This is a matter of the greatest importance for the Speaker, and I should regret it very much if the practice is not accepted as an obligation upon the House in every future Parliament. Having a team of four (including the Speaker) also means that a balance can be kept between Government and Opposition. Two can come from seats normally held by the Government and two from seats normally held by the Opposition. When a Government has a large majority, this does not matter, but in a narrowly balanced Parliament it is a factor to be taken into consideration.

I did all I could behind the scenes to see that the practice continued when George Thomas was elected my successor. After some doubts the main Parties agreed; Oscar Murton was elected Chairman of Ways and Means, Myer Galpern became First Deputy Chairman of Ways and Means and Godman Irvine, Conservative Member for Rye, became Second Deputy. That left the balance as before, two occupants of the Chair elected as Labour and two as Conservative Members.

With or without this Second Deputy Chairman of Ways

and Means and quite apart from the time spent in the Chair, I found the Speaker's day a very full one. As so much could not be delegated, my life during parliamentary sessions was more strenuous than it had been in any of the ministerial posts which I held (except at times of sudden crisis).

Some procedural matter would almost certainly have to be considered. I have already referred to most of them: rulings on privilege, matters sub judice, points of order of which I had had notice or on which I had deferred a decision, applications for emergency debates, P.N.Q.s and personal statements. Also there might be the selection of amendments. All these varied very much in their complexity, but on occasion they would require considerable study and thought.

Then there would be the selection of speakers. This involved reading all the letters from Members applying to speak, looking up their records in my Blue Book, perhaps making inquiries about their particular interests or their responsibilities on Select or Party Committees. I would make out a provisional order of calling, with notes so that the Deputies would understand my reasons.

Occasionally unusual problems would present themselves at short notice. The Stonehouse case was an example. He had been arrested on various charges in July 1975. He claimed the right, (or it was thought that he would claim it), to make a statement in person to the House. I ruled that while he was in custody he had no such right. It would need a resolution of the House, requiring the Court to make it possible for him to do so.

It is extremely important that the Speaker should maintain close contact with those who, to a large extent, control the business of the House. From time to time, formal letters had to be written to the Prime Minister, Leader of the House or Government Chief Whip, or on the other side to the Leader of the Opposition, the Shadow Leader of the House or Opposition Chief Whip. Apart from this formal correspondence, there was almost daily contact with the Chief Whips of the two big Parties. I would talk to them on the telephone or in person. I would almost always see them separately and talk in confidence. I would not pass on the thinking or plans of one side to the other unless authorized to do so. During the 1970–74 Parliament, the Chief Whips were Pym and then Humphrey Atkins for the Conservatives, and for the Opposition Mellish. For the rest of my time, Mellish was Government and Atkins Opposition Chief Whip respectively.

There were others concerned. In the time of the Conservative Government, the Leaders of the House were Willie Whitelaw, Robert Carr and Jim Prior in succession. During the Labour Government, Ted Short was Leader of the House, and John Peyton, Shadow Leader. There were also during my five years Jeremy Thorpe, David Steel and Cyril Smith for the Liberals, Donald Stewart and Douglas Henderson for the Scottish National Party (which I will in future call the S.N.P.), Harry West, James Molyneaux and Robert Bradford for the United Ulster Unionists (hereafter called U.U.U.) and Gwynfor Evans for Plaid Cymru.

Finally there were the personal contacts with Members. I used to encourage them to come and have a word with me in the Chair. As Members passed by during a division, I would talk to one or two, a Member who had been ill, or on a mission overseas or who had been involved in some incident. I felt it important to try to get on personal terms with all of them, to learn about their foibles, hobbies, domestic circumstances, strengths and weaknesses. In the last two Parliaments, time did not permit of my doing this with by any means all of them, but only a very few actually refused this kind of relationship.

Of course there was a constant trickle of complaints about not being called to speak or for a supplementary question. Only rarely did a Member insist on a personal interview. I never refused one, although because of the pressure on my time I did not encourage them.

All this was management of the House in the short term. In the longer term, there was also much to do.

In the 1970–74 Parliament, I announced on 2nd August 1972 the setting up of a Speaker's Conference on electoral law. It was agreed after protracted discussion that the Conference should consider the following matters: the franchise, particularly in relation to British subjects temporarily living abroad; registration; minimum age for election; election expenditure generally; conduct of elections, particularly in relation to some named matters and certain other problems.

The first Speaker's Conference had been set up in 1916 to consider (a) reform of the franchise, (b) a basis for redistribution of seats, (c) reform of the system of registration, (d) methods of elections, and the manner in which their costs should be borne. It was hoped that agreed solutions might emerge from this body, of which the Speaker was appointed chairman, and to whom was entrusted the task of selecting the members.

This Conference led to the enfranchisement of women aged over thirty, a simplification of the franchise, modification of the registration system, the redistribution of seats on an equitable basis, and the payment by a candidate of a £150 deposit, to be forfeited if he polled less than one eighth of the votes cast.

As Laundy puts it, 'In short the Speaker's Conference of 1916 led to the most sweeping electoral reforms since those introduced by the Reform Act in 1832. The comparative smoothness with which they were carried into effect spoke favourably for the method whereby the ground was prepared, namely the convening of a representative conference presided over by the very personification of aloof impartiality, Mr. Speaker.'

In 1929, what was called a Speaker's Conference was set up to consider electoral reform under the chairmanship of Lord Ullswater, who, as Speaker Lowther, had presided over the previous one in 1916. This failed to agree on any recommendations.

In 1944, another one was set up under Speaker Clifton Brown to consider redistribution, the franchise, conduct and cost of elections and methods of election. It overwhelmingly rejected proportional representation and the alternative vote. Its recommendations with regard to the business and university vote were rejected by the Government, but those with regard to the redistribution of seats were accepted.

In May 1965 a Conference was set up under Speaker Hylton-Foster to consider the voting age, methods of voting, the conduct of elections, election expenses, the use of broadcasting, and other matters. After Speaker Hylton-Foster's death, Speaker King took over in November 1965.

It made certain recommendations. With regard to the voting age, after many months of discussion a compromise recommendation was arrived at unanimously, except for one Member. Some wanted the age to remain at twenty-one; others wished it to come down to eighteen. The compromise age decided on was twenty. This was rejected by the Government and the age reduced to eighteen.

Certain recommendations of the Conference were accepted, such as those dealing with the residential qualification of merchant seamen; disenfranchisement of offenders in prison; extension for married persons of the right to vote by proxy or post; increase of the limit on candidates' election expenses; and broadcasting during elections.

The Conference over which I presided had twenty-nine other members. We met or tried to meet once a week. The average attendance was about half. A move to allow the Deputy Speaker to stand in for me from time to time was narrowly defeated.

I found it a very time-consuming and cumbersome operation. We were too large a body to consider some of the more detailed matters put to us. It was difficult to assemble the necessary evidence. We reported, in the form of letters from me to the Prime Minister, on certain minor matters in June, October and November 1973. We did, however, have one quite substantial achievement to our credit. In February 1974, a general election suddenly became imminent. The Conference had not yet dealt with election expenses. Owing to inflation, the rates then allowed meant that many candidates could not have conducted an election campaign even on a modest basis without breaking the law. I told the Conference on 6th February that if we could agree unanimously on increased rates within one hour, there was a sporting chance that the Government would legislate to implement our findings before Parliament was dissolved.

We reached agreement, with one or two grumbles, and reported that day. The Government accepted our recommendation. The Representation of the People Act 1974 was passed the following day, and most candidates were saved from almost inevitable breaches of the law.

I was glad that no attempt was made to set up another conference while I was Speaker. I think that there is advantage occasionally in a body presided over by the Speaker with his 'aloof impartiality'. But its methods of working need re-examination, and I have put forward my own suggestions in a later chapter.

The Speaker has to be concerned with the work of the Select Committees on Procedure. To set up such a committee, a resolution of the House is required. Sometimes they are given general orders of reference. Those set up in the 1967-8 and 1974-5 sessions had limited orders of reference. In the 1973-4 and 1974 sessions, no committee was appointed, and there were complaints from Members. When I left the Chair, one had not been appointed for that session.

When they had been set up, on occasion I gave oral evidence or submitted a memorandum; sometimes both. I had to study their reports carefully and read the evidence upon which they were based. During my time as Speaker successive committees reported upon a wide variety of topics. Some of them were purely House of Commons matters, such as the right of Members to attend meetings of Select Committees, the introduction of new Members after by-elections, late sittings and indeed the election of a Speaker. Others were of much more general interest, such as the scrutiny of taxation, debates on defence, European secondary legislation, and the process of legislation.

In March 1965 the Prime Minister announced that Her Majesty had graciously agreed that the control, use and occupation of the Palace of Westminster and its precincts should be permanently enjoyed by the Houses of Parliament. The Government had decided accordingly that the control of the accommodation and services in that part of the Palace and its precincts then occupied by or on behalf of the House of Commons should be vested in the Speaker of the House on behalf of that House.

Before that, supreme control was vested in the Lord Great Chamberlain. When the House of Commons was sitting, control was delegated on his behalf to the Serjeant at Arms acting on behalf of Mr Speaker. At week-ends and during recesses control reverted to the Lord Great Chamberlain. This was resented by some Members, and so the Palace was 'nationalized'.

A Select Committee of which I was a member recommended in July 1965 that a Sessional Select Committee, to be called the House of Commons Services Committee, should be appointed to advise Mr Speaker on the discharge of the new responsibilities vested in him. This was done. I was a member of it from its inception and chairman for a time in 1970. This experience was of great help to me when I became Speaker. I knew some of the difficulties in controlling a palace covering $10\frac{1}{2}$ acres, with 1,100 rooms, 2 miles of passages, 21 passenger lifts and 100 staircases. I was aware of the pitfalls awaiting the Kitchen Committee. I had spent many hours studying ways of increasing the accommodation available to Members. I knew what had been achieved in that respect. Recruiting of staff, expansion of the library, facilities for secretaries, parking, what could be photographed and where, visitors, the taping of proceedings to make up for the shortage of shorthand writers, the annunciator system, booking of rooms for meals, security in the Chamber, traffic lights in Parliament Square and a host of other matters had to some extent been within my knowledge. I knew that there were no easy solutions to most of the problems posed.

As Speaker, I had to be the final arbiter, and, strenuously as I sought to delegate, I found that most of the problems returned like old friends to make themselves known to me again.

On a normal working day my programme would be something like this.

From about 7.30 to 9 a.m., I would have breakfast, read the newspapers, and listen to the news on the radio. I had to do this thoroughly to find out what subjects might be raised later in the day by way of a P.N.Q. or an application under Standing Order No. 9 for an emergency debate.

At about 9.15 one of the Trainbearers would bring up my letters, the Order Paper and the Lords' and Commons' Hansards for the previous day.

At 9.45 Brigadier Short, my official secretary, would come with the day's programme. We would review the engagements; he would tell me about any visitors who might be coming during the day; we would discuss future engagements and visitors; we would decide how to handle anything which might have cropped up the day before, in other words how to handle a Member's complaint, or what official advice to seek; we would also consider the line I should take in the longer term on any of the administrative matters already mentioned.

At about 10.15 Miss Carter, my personal private secretary, would come to deal with constituency and unofficial correspondence. This would take about an hour. Then at

11.15 I would probably have a brief talk with Christopher Spence, my personal assistant. He had charge of my personal papers, records, diaries, and letters. He dealt with engagements in the constituency, travelling arrangements and entertainment.

At about 11.30 I would usually see someone, perhaps the Clerk, the Serjeant at Arms, a Member or an important visitor; I preferred however at this time, if possible, only to deal with matters relating to the House itself.

At noon, from Mondays to Thursdays, there would be the daily meeting of what was in fact my operations group. It would be attended by the Clerk, the Clerk Assistant and the Second Clerk Assistant (those are the three who sit in front of the Speaker in the Chamber in wig and gown), my Secretary, any of the Deputies who were free to come and any member of the Clerk's Department whom he wished to be present.

We would go through the business for the day, Private Business (affecting Private Bills) then questions, to ascertain whether there were special problems about any of them, for example the sub judice rule, and how the groupings, if any, had been arranged. After that we would consider any applications for P.N.Q.s, or applications under Standing Order No. 9. I would decide on the P.N.Q.s, and on the selection of amendments to motions. If the Report Stage of a Bill was being taken, I would select the amendments to be discussed. We would consider rulings on points of order raised the day before, or on matters of privilege. We would discuss the scope of debates, particularly on Statutory Instruments. At the end, I would probably have a word with the Deputies about the selection of speakers and possible snags.

After that meeting, I might have to deal with one or both Chief Whips on some point that had arisen, and I would almost certainly have an official visitor, probably a Speaker or leading Parliamentarian from abroad, or an Ambassador with a special message.

From 1 p.m. until 2.20, I would have to change into my official robes, tie up any loose ends about the day's business, have lunch, usually with my personal assistant, and discuss in more detail matters for which he was responsible.

At 2.20 I would go downstairs, put on my wig and gown, go to the outer office, and have a moment or two with the Serjeant at Arms and my chaplain.

We would then leave in procession to the Chamber. A Doorkeeper led the way, followed by the Serjeant at Arms with the Mace, then myself with a Trainbearer, and my chaplain and Secretary.

We would process along the Library corridor, past the Smoking Room. I could never resist looking in through that door for a fleeting glimpse of an old haunt. Then, as we turned right, a stentorian police voice would be heard crying out 'Hats off strangers', and we would go on through the main lobby. The Speaker's procession passing through the main lobby is a phenomenon that dates only from 1945. The Commons Chamber was still in ruins. The Lords had therefore handed over their Chamber to the Commons and themselves sat in the Royal Robing Room. To reach the Lords, the Speaker processed through the main lobby. It proved a popular attraction, and when the Commons' own Chamber was rebuilt and again in use, the Speaker continued the procession through the main lobby, turning right towards the Commons instead of left to the Lords.

From the main lobby, one came to the Members' lobby, where Members, ex-Members, and certain members of the Press are allowed to come. Until Speaker Denison's time, this had been like the main lobby, to which all and sundry could come provided they had a reason. In March 1870 Speaker Denison cleared them out of the Members' lobby, and limited them to the main lobby, obviously a wise and prescient step.

On our arrival in the Chamber at 2.30 p.m., the Chaplain read prayers. I would stay in the Chair for questions, P.N.Q.s, statements and the business of the day until

4.30. I would then leave the Chair for about two hours. After a cup of tea I would dispose of anything initiated earlier in the day, signing constituency and official letters and approving drafts. There would be the afternoon constituency post, and probably a Member, an official, and a visitor to be seen. Perhaps I would go for a short time to some party in or near the House.

From 6.30 to 7.30 I would be in the Chair again. From 7.30 to 9.15 or 9.30, I would be out of the Chair. The precise time of return would depend on whether there was some official dinner. I liked to be in the Chair for the final speech and at least part of the one preceding it, if it was likely to be a noisy affair. I would leave fairly soon after the vote, if there was one; perhaps one final visitor and then the day would be over.

This would be a normal day. If the House was sitting very late, or the Deputies had had a very hard time of it, I would sometimes go back to the Chair for a further stint, perhaps from 11.15 p.m. to midnight. If any other duties had to be fitted into the day — a State banquet, a memorial service, a speech to Commonwealth parliamentarians, taking the Chair at the Speaker's Conference or anything of that sort — the rest of the programme would have to be telescoped and some of it no doubt left over for the next day.

This sounds like and was an exacting day. But I had one constant pleasure. I lived in one of the most delightful flats in London.

Until I became Speaker I knew very little about his private apartments. Although I had been a Member for twenty-five years, I had never been in the Speaker's Residence until Speaker King asked me to dinner there in December 1970, after my candidature for Speaker had been endorsed by both the Cabinet and the Shadow Cabinet. This is not surprising or unusual. Frequently I had been entertained by my predecessors on official occasions in the State Rooms, but I had not been on terms of private friendship with any of them, although we had been good friends in the parliamentary sense. Any personal talks had always been in the Speaker's Library on the principal floor.

Speaker's House used to be a residence on a grand scale, the ground floor consisting of large kitchens, store-rooms, and no doubt some staff quarters. A fine staircase leads from Speaker's Court to the first or principal floor, on which are the State Rooms, consisting of a large dining-room with a long table at which thirty-six people can dine in comfort, a large drawing-room, and two smaller ones, with doors leading from each one to the next. There was also a large library. Above the principal floor were the main bedrooms, dressing-rooms and bathrooms. Above that floor were various rooms of miscellaneous shapes and sizes, with many steps to be mounted to get to them, the whole designed to fit into the structure created by Sir Charles Barry, which looks so grand from Westminster Bridge. It certainly was not purpose-built. It needed a large indoor staff to run the place—in Speaker FitzRoy's time about a dozen, so his son told me.

In these less spacious days, almost the whole of the cellar floor, together with the Speaker's Library, has been handed over to the House of Commons Library. The State Rooms are as before. But because the Speaker has to use one of the smaller drawing-rooms, instead of the Library, as a study or personal office, the drawing-room from the Serjeant at Arms' house, next to the Speaker's dining-room, has now been added to Speaker's House.

The Speaker's private accommodation is limited to the principal bedroom floor. That is now the Speaker's Residence, and has been since Speaker Clifton Brown's time. It is in a magnificent position, overlooking the river, the Lords' and Commons' terraces, with views of Lambeth Palace, St Thomas's Hospital, the Greater London Council building, the Festival Hall, Somerset House, the Savoy Hotel, and other well-known buildings. When I took possession, there were comfortably sized dining- and sitting-rooms, a small study, four bedrooms, a dressing-room and two bathrooms. In addition there were what had at some time been staff quarters—two bedrooms, a small sitting-room, a bathroom and a kitchen, with a beautiful view down the river, but an unsightly cupboard larder and some very out-of-date kitchen equipment.

Except in the staff quarters, the oak had been bleached. The furniture varied in quality; in one bedroom there was an enormous Pugin wardrobe which took up about a third of the room.

The whole floor had obviously been converted from a bedroom floor into a self-contained residence at a time of serious shortages. The materials then available had suffered with the passage of time. There had been other pressing calls upon resources. But I felt that the time had come for a major effort. From my time at the Foreign Office and the Treasury, I knew how helpful the Office of Works could be. With their willing help under their new name, over a period of about three years I managed to make some considerable improvements. The kitchen was completely redesigned, the cupboard larder removed and modern equipment installed. The dressing-room was turned into a bathroom leading out of my bedroom, with cupboards for clothes. The other bathrooms were modernized. The bedrooms were redecorated. The Pugin wardrobe was removed, although I imposed the condition that it must be found a home elsewhere. I was also lent some attractive pictures. After these changes I claimed, I think with good cause, that it was the best 'tied cottage' in London.

Apart from the Residence, I succeeded in having some improvements made on the principal floor. I found there only one lavatory for men, and one for women. It had been so for a hundred years or more. When I had my receptions for the Diplomatic Corps with five hundred guests, I shuddered to think of the 'inconvenience'. After three years the facilities for men were increased fivefold and those for women doubled. The space available made it impossible to do more at reasonable cost.

The extent to which the Speaker entertains privately is a matter for him to decide. To a large degree it depends upon his financial resources. Speaker Addington's emoluments in 1789 were £6,000 a year and, in addition to certain allowances, two hogsheads of claret per annum. I am told that a hogshead is 344 bottles. To give a modern Speaker a salary with equivalent purchasing power after tax, would require an astronomic sum. He now receives the same salary as a Cabinet Minister, but with some allowances in addition, which are helpful.

Owing to the impartiality of the Chair, Speaker's House provides an admirable neutral meeting ground for those with widely different views. I started off with the idea of having all Members to lunch. In my first two Parliaments, I entertained about five hundred in this way. Eight of us would sit down, myself and seven others. I would have three from each of the two major Parties, one new-comer, one with several years experience of the House and one old timer. The seventh would be a Liberal or Independent Member or an official. The lunches were provided by the Refreshment Department, and we used to eat at an octagonal table in the small State drawing-room. These lunches were extremely valuable to me for keeping in touch with the feelings of back-benchers, and for getting to know younger Members and their first impressions of the House. Latterly, much to my regret, rising costs forced me to reduce their frequency, but had I remained as Speaker for the whole of my third Parliament, I would have found ways of continuing them.

In addition I began by trying about every two months to have an evening party for a widely drawn mixture of guests. I invited Members of Parliament, peers, officials, industrialists, representatives of the political parties, trade unionists, business and personal friends. However, these parties were not wholly successful. Too many of the people

I really wanted to get to meet one another were overwhelmed with other engagements.

I also decided that I would give an annual reception for the Diplomatic Corps, inviting all Ambassadors and High Commissioners and their wives, the Cabinet and Shadow Cabinet, Members with particular interest in foreign affairs, and our own retired Ambassadors and High Commissioners, most of whom I had known during my time at the Foreign Office. The first one was in March 1972 and seemed to be a great success. When the day came for the second one in March 1973, a railway strike was in progress, and at about 3 p.m. in the afternoon several bombs exploded in the Whitehall area. Nevertheless, 480 people succeeded in making their way to Speaker's House. Owing to the general election in February 1974, I did not give one that year.

It has been the custom that immediately after the State Opening of Parliament, the Speaker should give a party for leading Members of the two Houses, the senior Ambassadors, and other distinguished guests. In 1974 and 1975 I increased the size of this party because I had not given the reception for the Diplomatic Corps. About 130 guests came on each occasion.

In December 1972 Queen Elizabeth the Queen Mother came to dine. I invited nine Conservative Members, nine Labour and one Liberal to meet her, and after dinner between twenty and thirty other Members came in. In November 1973 the Prince of Wales came to a cocktail party for the Welsh Members of all Parties and their wives.

From time to time I was also asked to entertain a visiting Head of State who particularly wished to come to the House of Commons. The Queen of the Netherlands, the King of Afghanistan and the President of the West German Federal Republic were among those who visited Speaker's House.

Each summer the Speaker has his tea parties and all

Members and their wives or husbands are invited, as well as others concerned with the work of the House.

There were various gatherings for some of the charitable bodies with which I had been connected, Task Force, the Young Volunteer Force Foundation and the Home Farm Trust. The English-Speaking Union on one occasion asked me to entertain American visitors. Twice Rugby League supporters came on the eve of their Cup Final at Wembley, and we had most enjoyable parties with them and their Members of Parliament. There would be something of this sort two or three times a year, each with about seventy guests.

In addition there were many opportunities to offer hospitality in a smaller and more casual way. I had many of the leading parliamentary figures to small dinners in my flat. Almost every day there were several individual visitors coming to see me for some reason or another. There were also many parties of varying sizes for my own friends.

All this was my private hospitality. I would like to have done much more, had not costs risen so sharply.

Apart from what I have described, many functions took place in Speaker's House for which I myself was not financially responsible. Her Majesty the Queen and Prince Philip came to Speaker's House after the opening of the Inter-Parliamentary Union Conference in September 1975 to meet the leading delegates. In December 1975 the Prince of Wales dined as the guest of the Commonwealth Parliamentary Association. They were noteworthy occasions. The Lord Chancellor and I were nominal hosts. But on this sort of occasion the expense was born either by the Government or by a body such as the Inter-Parliamentary Union or the Commonwealth Parliamentary Association. The same rule applied to dinners for visiting delegations or members of other Parliaments or Assemblies. Their scale and frequency were such that appropriate entertainment was far beyond the Speaker's personal resources.

Some think that when the House is not sitting, the

Speaker is on holiday. This is not so. Apart from constituency engagements, I had to undertake a number of other duties. During my five years as Speaker I went to Japan, Iran, Finland, Rumania and Yugoslavia on official visits. In Tokyo I opened an exhibition informing the Japanese about the British Parliament. The visits to the other four countries were as the guest of their Speakers. In each there was a strenuous but enjoyable programme of engagements, courtesy calls, discussions with Ministers and Parliamentarians and sight-seeing. There was quite a lot of speech-making. I went to Belfast for the fiftieth anniversary of the Stormont Parliament. I attended a meeting in Strasbourg of the Presiding Officers of various European Chambers of Deputies.

In addition there were some great occasions in London during the long recess, including the visit of the American Bar Association and the Annual Conference of the Inter-Parliamentary Union, at the commencement of each of which the Queen was present in Westminster Hall. Both involved a number of official engagements for the Speaker.

# V

# The Speaker Seeking
# Re-election

When I accepted nomination for the Speakership in January 1971, I had not given a thought to what would happen at the next general election.

The last election, won by the Conservatives, had been on 20th June 1970. This meant that, at the furthest stretch, the next general election need not be held until July 1975. I would by then have been Speaker for four and a half years. If I stood again and was re-elected Speaker, I could not subject my constituents to a by-election for at least twelve months. That meant my remaining Speaker until I was seventy-three. That, I felt, would be too long, and I should have had to consider resigning during or at the end of the 1970 Parliament. On the other hand, if the election were in October 1974, the traditional month, I should have been Speaker for only three years and nine months. I would probably wish to seek re-election.

In the event I did not have to make any such difficult decision. On 7th February 1974, Mr Heath announced his intention of going to the country, with polling day on 28th February.

Then began the tenth election campaign of my career and the strangest.

The difficulty lay in explaining in sufficiently clear terms the unique position of the Speaker: why, on election as

Speaker, he had to become non-party; why he had to
be re-elected as an M.P.; whether, if he was, he would be
re-elected Speaker; whether voters in Wirral were voting
for him as M.P. or Speaker or both. Quite a number thought
that I would continue as Speaker, even if defeated in the
fight to continue as M.P.

An additional problem was the substantial change since
1970 in the boundaries of my constituency. The Upton
and Prenton wards of Birkenhead had taken the place of
the municipal borough of Ellesmere Port, with whose
Labour leaders I had had cordial relations throughout
my twenty-five years' membership for the Port.

The newly constituted Wirral Labour Party announced
its intention of opposing me, on the grounds that Wirral
was in effect a new constituency, and that the voters should
have the chance to say whether they wanted me or someone
else as their Member. There was a precedent for this,
although I did not know it at the time and I doubt whether
my Labour opponent did. The Conservatives opposed
Speaker Peel in the general election at the end of 1885 on
the same grounds. In 1880 he had been returned as a
Liberal for the borough of Warwick. By the Redistribution
Act of 1885, Leamington had been incorporated with
Warwick into a new constituency. The Conservatives
maintained that the political opinions of that new constituency should be tested.

I had looked up other precedents. Peel was re-elected
in 1885, and not opposed in 1886 or 1892. He retired in
1895 shortly before an expected general election. Gully, a
Liberal, was put up by the Liberals to succeed him. I have
already described (page 57) the Conservative opposition
to him when he was proposed as Speaker, and also in his
constituency of Carlisle at the following general election.

During that election, Gully decided to address a public
meeting, and, to quote from Laundy,

while making no reference to the political issues on

which the election was being fought, he stated his views as to why the Speaker should not be opposed when seeking re-election, 'The first reason was that the English people were in the main lovers of fair play, and that it had struck them as being a somewhat unfair spectacle to see someone who, in the public interest, was disabled from protecting himself by the ordinary weapons of political warfare, exposed to an attack and unable to defend himself. A Speaker could not withdraw from the political arena. On the contrary, he must be a Member before he was a Speaker, but he was disarmed. It had occurred to our fathers and forefathers that it was unfair to put a man disarmed in the middle of a ring, and that the proper course was not to subject him to the conditions of a contest. That appeared to some people of the present day to be a quixotic piece of generosity. He hoped there would be some generosity left still in public life.'

In an election in which the Liberals as a party were heavily defeated, Gully was re-elected with a majority increased from 143 to 314. As I have said, the victorious Conservatives made amends when the House met by themselves proposing him for re-election to the Chair.

Gully retired in 1905. Lowther, a Conservative who had been Deputy Speaker and Chairman of Ways and Means for ten years, was elected to succeed him without opposition. He was not opposed at the ensuing general election, and in spite of a sweeping victory for the Liberals, they supported his re-election as Speaker.

The same pattern continued for another thirty years. Lowther was not opposed in either election of 1910, or in 1918. Speaker Whitley (a Liberal) was not opposed in 1922, 1923 or 1924. His successor, FitzRoy (a Conservative) was not opposed in 1929 or 1931.

In 1935, however, the Labour Party announced its intention of opposing Speaker FitzRoy. Thereupon the

Conservatives and Liberals of Daventry unanimously adopted him as their non-party candidate. The figures were FitzRoy 18,934, Barnes (Labour) 10,767—majority 8,167. In his last contested election as a Conservative in 1924, his majority had been 200. The Labour Party defended its action on the ground that they were opposed to the principle of the Speaker representing a constituency like any other Member.

Speaker Clifton Brown was similarly opposed by a Labour candidate in 1945. The result was Clifton Brown 16,431, Kavanagh (Labour) 11,786—majority 4,645. In 1950, the Speaker was not opposed by a Labour candidate but by a gentleman describing himself as an Independent Liberal. The result was Clifton Brown 24,703, Hancock (Ind. Lib.) 4,154—majority 20,549.

As Speaker Clifton Brown had resigned at the end of the 1950–51 Parliament, there was no Speaker seeking re-election in the election of October 1951. At the next one, in May 1955, Speaker Morrison stood as the Speaker seeking re-election. Attlee, the leader of the Labour Party, appeared by then to have had second thoughts about his Party's line, and he wrote this letter to Speaker Morrison, 'In accordance with the time honoured custom of not contesting the Speaker's seat, the Labour Party has no candidate in the Cirencester and Tewkesbury constituency. Labour supporters are urged to observe this British political tradition.' The Liberal leader, Clement Davies, sent a similar message.

Nevertheless an independent Labour candidate stood. The result was Morrison 25,372, Cox (Ind. Lab.) 12,394—majority 12,978.

Speaker Morrison resigned at the end of that Parliament and in the 1959 election there was no Speaker seeking re-election. In October 1964, however, Speaker Hylton-Foster had to face a three-cornered contest. Both the Labour and Liberal Parties put up official candidates against him. The result was Hylton-Foster 21,588, Wallace

(Lab.) 11,309, Derry (Lib.) 4,087 — majority 10,279. The Speaker's share of the poll had gone down from 65·1 per cent, standing as a Conservative in 1959, to 58·4 per cent. None the less it was an impressive victory for a candidate who could not campaign for himself.

Hylton-Foster died in 1965. Horace King was elected Speaker in his place, and in March 1966 he had to face an election in his Southampton Itchen seat which he had held by a majority of 9,975 in a three-cornered fight in October 1964. The Conservative and Liberal Parties decided not to oppose him, but an independent Democratic Non-Party Nationalist did stand. The result was King 30,463, Hunt (Dem. Non-Party Nat.) 5,217 — majority 25,246. In the General Election of June 1970, the Conservative and Liberal Parties again decided not to oppose Horace King, but this time two independents stood. The result was King 29,417, Bray (Nat. Dem.) 9,581, Phillips (Ind.) 4,794 — majority 19,836.

In Horace King's election address for that election he wrote,

> A vote for the Speaker is not a vote for any political party. It is a vote for a man who, following the traditions of his office, cannot make public speeches, indeed who can do nothing to defend himself at a General Election. He must, simply, leave it to the voters of his constituency to see fair play.
>
> Because of these restrictions a tradition has grown up that the Speaker's re-election to Parliament is not opposed by the main political parties at a General Election.
>
> This tradition has been described as 'one of the finer and better traditions of English public life' and I deeply appreciate the honour which the Conservative and the Liberal Parties have once again done to the office of Mr. Speaker in not contesting the Speaker's seat.

As the campaign developed in Wirral in February 1974, the arguments of the Labour candidate were clear. In addition to making the point about the constituency having changed, he said that I ought to campaign as a Conservative; it was a denial of democratic rights for me not to be opposed in a constituency of the size of Wirral. Anyhow, he asked, who had laid down these rules about it being unfair to oppose the Speaker?

The Liberals informed me politely that as Labour were opposing me, they felt that they must do the same.

The Wirral Conservative Association, not unexpectedly, resolved not to put forward a Conservative candidate and asked their members to support me.

Although most senior members of the Labour and Liberal Parties at Westminster with whom I had discussed the matter told me privately that they thoroughly disapproved of the Speaker being opposed when seeking re-election in his constituency, I knew that they could not overrule their local party organizations.

I had therefore expected a fight and given much thought to the problems of conducting a campaign which could not be an ordinary political campaign. Clearly I could do very little myself. Equally clearly my supporters, who had worked hard for twenty-five years to have me returned as their Conservative Member, had no intention of allowing me to be ousted in favour of a Labour or Liberal opponent.

My first decision was about an agent. No serious candidate can fight an election without an agent—there are too many technicalities. During my time as Member for Wirral, I had been extremely fortunate. Bert Gill had been my agent in the five elections from 1945 to 1959. Then his health failed. His successor was Gilbert Stevenson, also very experienced, who had carried me through the 1964, 1966 and 1970 campaigns. He willingly agreed to act for me in February 1974. There was no legal or political difficulty about this as the choice of an election agent is a personal one for the candidate. He arranged for my nomination papers to be signed and organized the constituency into areas, each with what we called 'an officer in charge', some men and some women.

A canvass had to be arranged on my behalf. I agreed to have 40,000 copies of a leaflet printed for the canvassers to distribute. It contained no reference to party politics but explained the duties of the Speaker and the limitations imposed upon him, by convention, in an election campaign.

Then there was the problem of an election address. Clearly some communication had to be sent to every voter, again referring only to my position as Speaker, and to my interest in my Wirral constituents. Bands of voluntary workers were needed to address the envelopes. Mr Stevenson had to arrange this with the officers in charge.

Another problem also arose. What were to be my colours? I ventured to ask whether I needed to have any colours. I was put in my place at once. There were the posters, car stickers, rosettes and all the rest of it. My supporters accepted that I could not run under blue, the Conservative colours. Black would be too funereal for all of this. I chose green, the colour of the House of Commons benches, as opposed to the red in the Lords.

After I had made those decisions, there began my strangest election campaign. My first had been nearly forty-five years ago; there had been a further eight between 1945 and 1970. Since I had been in the Cabinet, my appearances in Wirral had been cut down to three or four days each campaign, to enable me to visit as many other constituencies as possible — in 1970 about thirty-five.

Thus after twenty-nine years as Member, I was obliged to spend the whole election in Wirral, but not allowed to make speeches, to canvass or to conduct the campaign. I was not to have a sticker on my car or even a poster in my garden.

We had settled the problems of the appointment of an agent, the introductory leaflet, the election address, the officers in charge, the addressing of the envelopes and the canvassing.

That was all very well, but what on earth was I to do myself? It was brought home to me that the candidate's personal endeavours during a campaign (provided he is already well known) are comparatively unimportant. I did my shopping on a modest scale; I went to my Church; I attended one or two non-party occasions; I was photographed incessantly, usually in the coldest possible place; I gave television and radio interviews whenever I was asked; I went round thanking the helpers addressing envelopes and putting the election addresses into them. But throughout the whole campaign, I never once myself asked anyone to vote for me. I did, however, agree to visit the polling stations and my committee rooms on polling day.

There were compensations. Some Labour and Liberal supporters said that they regretted that I was being opposed. In a crowded shopping centre, a man employed by a nationalized industry which I will not name, a notorious left-winger, jumped off his bicycle and shouted 'Good luck Selwyn—I hate the Tories but I think it's a bloody shame you're being opposed.'

I was not in serious doubt as to the result. The support from the three-fifths of the constituency which I had represented for so long was solidly based, and with the new two-fifths I think that I maintained something not far short of the ratio of fifty–fifty between my supporters and my opponents, as shown in the final result.

It was very satisfactory: Lloyd 38,452, Whipp (Labour) 22,605, Gayford (Liberal) 14,123—majority 15,847. My share of the poll was 51·1 per cent compared with 55·1 per cent in 1970 and 48·1 per cent in 1966.

In October 1974 the campaign was conducted on much the same lines and the result was Lloyd 35,705, Thomas (Labour) 22,217, Gayford (Liberal) 12,345—majority 13,488. This time on a reduced poll my share of the poll was 50·8 per cent, a decline of 0·3 per cent, which did not greatly disconcert me.

In this second election, my Liberal opponent placed much more emphasis on the issue that the electors of Wirral were being disenfranchised by having the Speaker as their Member, and that there ought to be a special or fictitious seat for the Speaker.

He and his supporters also made great play with the fact that on the occasion already referred to (page 73) I had given my casting vote for the Government on an Opposition amendment to the Trade Union and Labour Relations Bill. My Liberal opponent in his election address said 'the Speaker had to vote with the Labour Government when there was a dead heat'. It was difficult to nail this inaccurate statement, and to convince people that had the amendments been Labour Government amendments, I would in accordance with precedent have voted against them. My opponents also failed to mention that the Deputy Speakers also do not vote or speak in the Commons—no special or fictitious seats were suggested for them.

I did my best to see that my election literature dealt with these criticisms, and there was some acrimonious correspondence in the local press between my supporters and those of the Liberal candidate.

This is perhaps a convenient place to examine the argument that the Speaker ought to have a special or fictitious seat. Both Labour and Liberal conferences have passed resolutions to this effect without much discussion, if any. The case has not been argued out or indeed seriously considered since a Select Committee was set up in December 1938 to report on the matter.

Its terms of reference were to 'consider what steps if any should be taken to ensure that, having due regard to the constitutional rights of the electors, the Speaker, during his continuance in office, shall not be required to take part in a contested parliamentary election'.

Its membership was impressive: for the Labour Party

Mr Clynes, Mr Lansbury, Mr Stephen, Mr Denman, Mr Thorne and Sir Robert Young; for the Liberals Mr David Lloyd George, Sir Percy Harris and Mr George Lambert; for the Conservatives Mr Winston Churchill, Captain Bullock, Sir George Courthope, Sir Henry Page Croft, Mr McCorquodale, Captain McEwen and Sir Hugh O'Neill.

Mr Lloyd George was elected Chairman. The Committee's considerations went rather wider than the terms of reference. The conclusions of 14th April 1939 were unanimous.

The Committee rejected any interference with the right of electors to oppose the Speaker. They dealt fully and carefully with the argument that the Speaker's special position disenfranchises his constituents. They were not impressed by this point and said,

> In the British political system, whatever may be its merits or demerits, there is a strong party control over the actions of members in the House and the sterilization of a single vote on whichever side it might have been delivered will have so small an influence on matters which are the subject of party divisions as to be entirely negligible (para. 37).

They could have added that if the Deputy Speaker came from a different Party, the balance between Government and Opposition would remain unaltered, since he, like the Speaker, does not vote.

The Committee also dealt with the argument that the Speaker cannot by political means seek to redress the grievances of his constituents. They reported,

> In matters of individual interest or grievance the Speaker's constituents are in fact in a peculiarly favoured position. Though the Speaker himself can put down no questions, any matter affecting them which he feels justified in raising privately with a

Department of State will in the nature of human reactions, coming from such a source, receive the most careful consideration. Again if the circumstances of a particular case require that a question should receive public expression it would be, and in fact is, willingly sponsored by other Members. (para. 38)

As an alternative to the present system, the Committee examined the idea of a separate or special constituency for the Speaker, perhaps called St Stephen's. They concluded that its attractiveness was mainly superficial and that the more closely its implications were examined, the less agreeable did they become. They reported,

A Speaker elected by any such device and so removed from direct contact with a real electorate, the winning of whose confidence permitted him to enter the House of Commons, must in the process of time become increasingly divorced from the interests and vicissitudes of those over whom he presides. A deep sense of fellowship lies at the very root of those powers with which all Members to-day willingly clothe their chosen Speaker, and if this were lost, much of what now upholds his authority would of necessity go with it. It is not so many decades since the attitude of the House towards guidance from the Chair was markedly different from that adopted by all sides to-day; and it is not too much to say that this change is due to that widened sense of fellowship which could only develop under a strictly non-political Speakership. If this scheme were adopted, your Committee feel convinced that the proper aloofness of the Speaker from the political actions of Members would in time deteriorate into the detachment of the official. (para. 52)

Finally they concluded, 'To alter the status of the Speaker so that he ceased to be returned to the House of Commons

by the same electoral methods as other Members, or as a
representative of a parliamentary constituency would be
repugnant to the custom and tradition of the House.'
(para. 60)

I agreed entirely with the findings of that Committee,
and repeat what I have already said or implied.

An independent and impartial Speaker is an essential
element in our constitutional machinery. Since about
1834 when the impartiality of the Speaker was acknowledged,
more and more powers, discretions and responsibilities have
been heaped upon him. Except for the Prime Minister,
who can ask for a dissolution of Parliament, it may be
argued that the Speaker has more influence than any other
single Member over the way in which the House functions.
There are some democratic freedoms of which he is the sole
protector. For seven hundred years he has been an ordinary
Member of the House, summoned or elected as other
Members.

If he is in conflict with the House or a majority of it,
he can, as an ultimate resort, vacate the Chair, return
to the back-benches and argue his case from there. The
House of Commons cannot get rid of him (except by a
motion for expulsion which on a constitutional or political
issue would be inconceivable). Only his constituents can
dismiss him, at an election.

I reminded the House of this in my farewell as Speaker.
I said that I firmly believed that he should be elected as
other Members are, so that he can be in personal contact
with a body of constituents, and an area of the country.
I continued with what the *Daily Telegraph* described as
characteristic *jeu d'esprit*, 'To mark the fact that I am an
ordinary Member, I have decided, as is my right, to stay
on as a Member of this House.' (Hon. Members: 'Hear,
hear.') 'I am grateful for that response. I have also noticed
the uneasiness on the surfaces of the usual channels at the
prospect of having yet another floating voter. Although I
shall stay on, it will be only for a few days.'

If this system is altered, a fundamental blow will be struck at the Speakership. If by some resolution of the House the Speaker becomes a notional Member for a fictitious constituency, it would gravely diminish his authority and standing. He would soon have only the status of an official of the House without a corresponding security of tenure.

In conducting the business of the House, moreover, the Speaker should be familiar with what ordinary people are thinking, by letters from those whose homes and backgrounds he knows, and by personal contacts with them.

There is a final point. The Commons can function only if certain of its Members accept self-denying ordinances. Government Whips hardly ever speak in the House; Parliamentary Private Secretaries do not speak on matters affecting the Departments of the Ministers whom they serve; members of the Chairmen's Panel, who have taken the chair of a Standing Committee during the Committee Stage of a Bill do not speak (or vote) during the Report Stage or Third Reading of that Bill; the Chairman and the two Deputy Chairmen of Ways and Means do not speak or vote. If the Speaker is to be given a special constituency, what about the Deputy Speaker, and these others? Should not they have special seats? Where would it end?

There is a final point, which I add only because I am no longer Speaker, and the words are those of Mr Lloyd George's Committee, 'It cannot be disputed that a great honour is conferred on the constituency whose Member is chosen from among all others for those rare qualities which will enable him to fulfil the high office of presiding over the deliberations of the House of Commons.' (para. 38)

# VI

# Re-election as Speaker

The country went to the polls on Thursday, 28th February 1974. My Wirral result was declared for the eighth and, because of the constituency changes, the last time from a platform outside the Central Hall in Market Street, Hoylake.

My recollection is that I drove up to Speaker's House some time on Monday, 4th March, when it was apparent that the talks between the Conservatives and Liberals were not going well, and that Harold Wilson would probably that day be called upon to form a Government. As I came into Speaker's Court, Mellish, the Labour Chief Whip, was just getting out of his car. I went across to have a word with him. The substance of the conversation was that his Party would support my re-election as Speaker. If they had to find the Deputy Speaker, what did I think of George Thomas? Some weeks earlier, before the election campaign, this possibility had been mentioned to me by Harold Wilson. I replied that I would welcome very much indeed Thomas's appointment as Deputy Speaker.

The new Parliament met at 2.30 p.m. on Wednesday, 6th March.

The procedure for the election of the Speaker was in several ways quite different from what had happened on 12th January 1971, partly because this time the election was taking place at the beginning of a new Parliament and partly because the recommendations of the Procedure

Committee with regard to the Election of a Speaker had been largely adopted. The Committee had considered the matter as a result of the criticisms made at the time of my first election. It reported to the House on 26th January 1972. Following upon the Report, a new Standing Order (No. 103A) was adopted. Its general effect was that,

(1) If Mr Speaker ceased for any reason to be a Member of the House, the Chair should be taken for the election of a new one by the Member, not being a Minister, who had served continuously for the longest period.

(2) If Mr Speaker signified his wish to relinquish his office, he should continue to take the Chair until a new Speaker had been chosen, whereupon Mr Speaker-Elect should take the Chair.

(3) The Member taking the Chair in the circumstances set out in (1) above should have all the Speaker's powers.

(4) On a motion that a certain Member take the Chair as Speaker, the question should be proposed on that motion, and the question on any further motion (i.e., an alternative name) should be put as an amendment to that motion.

This new Standing Order met some of the criticisms put forward in the debate on 12th January 1971, and rescued the Clerk of the House from the somewhat invidious position of having to take the Chair without any power at all to invoke the Standing Orders.

I had ceased to be a Member on the dissolution of the previous Parliament, although remaining Speaker, but I had not signified my wish to relinquish my office. Accordingly the procedure under (1) above was followed.

George Strauss, Labour Member for Lambeth, Vauxhall, was the new Father of the House. He had first stood in 1924 for Lambeth (North) and had lost by twenty-nine votes. He won the seat in 1929, lost it in the 1931 landslide, but won it back at a by-election in 1934 and had been a Member ever since.

A further difference from January 1971 was that this time the Parliamentary Labour Party had been informed during the morning of 6th March that it was the Government's intention to support me, and that, as I was subsequently told, there had been no dissentient voices.

The formalities began with the Trainbearer placing the Mace under the Table shortly before 2.30 p.m., having entered the Chamber from behind the Chair. He then conducted me to the corner seat in the third row above the gangway on the Government side. I was surrounded by friendly Labour Members delighted to be sitting on that side. John Parker, Labour Member for Dagenham since 1935, had agreed to propose me, and Derek Walker-Smith, a Conservative Member since 1945, was to second me.

I and those near me could not see John Parker, and when I said that it looked as though he had failed to turn up, Willie Hamilton, who had opposed my election in 1971 and who was squatting in the gangway beside me said 'Don't worry, if he doesn't turn up, I'll propose you myself.' Parker, in fact, was there.

At the appointed hour, the Clerk of the Crown in Chancery in Great Britain, Sir Denis Dobson, delivered to Mr David Lidderdale (as he then was), the Clerk of the House, the book containing the list of the Members returned to serve in the new Parliament. I have often wondered what possible way there can be of checking that list and ensuring that there are no strangers among those who crowd into the Chamber on the first day.

Then George Strauss took the Chair according to the Standing Order. Black Rod came to summon the Commons to the Lords to hear the commission read for the opening and holding of the Parliament and the direction 'to proceed to the Election of a Speaker and to present him tomorrow at half-past two o'clock in the House of Peers for the Royal approbation'.

Strauss led the procession with Black Rod on his right. I remained in the House, with most other Members.

On his return, Strauss called on Parker. He proposed me, and after him Walker-Smith seconded me. Both made friendly speeches. I then spoke, submitting myself to the judgment of the House. The Question that I should take the Chair as Speaker was put and agreed to, and I was then 'taken out' of my place and conducted to the Chair. This time I put up rather more resistance according to the convention, my proposer and seconder being rather younger than Irene Ward and Charles Pannell had been in 1971.

I expressed my thanks. The Mace was placed upon the Table. Speeches of congratulation were made by Harold Wilson, Heath, Thorpe and Strauss, all very kind. The House then adjourned until the next day. Parker had begun his speech at 2.50. The House adjourned at 3.26.

On the following day, I went in procession, to the Chamber by the usual route, wearing a bobtailed wig but no gown. I was preceded by two Doorkeepers, the Serjeant at Arms (carrying the Mace across his left arm) and the Deputy Serjeant at Arms. I was followed by the Speaker's Secretary. There were no prayers.

I took the Chair. The summons came from the Lords. I went there again in procession, the Serjeant at Arms still carrying the Mace across his left arm.

The customary exchanges then took place, but, because it was the beginning of a Parliament, not in quite the same terms as those on 12th January 1971, described on pages 27–8.

After I had laid claim to all the ancient rights and privileges of the House of Commons, and when the Lord Chancellor had intimated the Queen's confirmation of them, I returned to the Commons' Chamber, passed through it to the small room behind the Speaker's Chair, put on my full-bottomed wig and my gown, and then came back into the Chair.

I then said,

I have to report to the House that, in the House of

Peers, Her Majesty, by Her Royal Commissioners, has been pleased to approve the choice made of myself for the Office of Speaker, and that I have, in your name and on your behalf, made claim by humble Petition to Her Majesty to all your ancient and undoubted rights and privileges—particularly to the freedom of speech in debate, freedom from arrest, freedom of access to Her Majesty whenever occasion may require, and that the most favourable construction may be placed upon all your proceedings. All these Her Majesty, by Her Commissioners, has been pleased to confirm in as ample a manner as they have ever been granted or confirmed by Herself or by any of Her Royal Predecessors.

My first duty to the House is to repeat my very respectful acknowledgments and my grateful thanks for the great honour you have conferred upon me in placing me in the Chair.

I then took the oath of allegiance standing on the steps up to the Chair. Members were sworn in one by one and presented to me in the Chair by the Clerk. I shook hands and said a word or two of greeting, usually light-hearted— 'So you have got here at last', 'Glad to see you've scraped in again'; 'Good Heavens, I thought we'd seen the last of you'. They were all so pleased to be re-elected, that they would have put up with almost anything.

## VII

# My Three Parliaments
# as Speaker

In each of these three Parliaments, the House of Commons was a very different place.

The first Parliament lasted from 29th June 1970 to 8th February 1974. I was Speaker for just over three years of that time. It was a bitter Parliament. Labour leaders and their followers gave the impression that they had not expected to be beaten and that they rather resented the decision of the electorate.

The new Government embarked on a programme of formidable proportions. Two large new Ministries were created. The Secretary of State for the Environment was given control over housing, transport, planning, local-government affairs, public works and many other matters as well. The Secretary of State for Trade and Industry was given control over trade, fuel and power, regional industrial development, aviation and shipping, and the sponsorship of most private industry.

There were major changes in the tax system, including unified income tax and surtax. VAT was introduced. However logical in theory, and necessary if we were to join the Common Market, it produced practical difficulties, particularly for small businesses.

The Industrial Relations Bill was presented. The Labour Party, strongly backed by the T.U.C., bitterly opposed it from the very beginning. I have already described some of the scenes in the House. It made difficult any kind of consensus approach to industrial relations.

The Bill was given a Second Reading by 324 votes to 280, the Liberals voting with the Government. It took many hours in Committee of the whole House, and a time-table motion was necessary. Once the Bill was through and the Industrial Court set up, there was a running stream of criticism of that Court, extending from failure to acknowledge its considerable conciliatory successes to open defiance. All this presented serious problems for the Chair. I have dealt with the difficulty of issues being sub judice elsewhere (pages 104–6).

In the economic field, the need for an incomes policy of some sort was soon appreciated by the Government, although some of their supporters maintained their disenchantment with the prospect. Government attempts to enforce such a policy in the public sector resulted in a confrontation with the miners in the mid-winter of 1971–2. Whatever the rights and wrongs, this strike created in the House not just criticism and resentment but an undertone of bitterness and almost hatred. Sympathy with miners working at the coal-face, the mass picketing which prevented supplies getting through to the power stations; the strain on the police and the public; the spirit of the miners and their loyalty to one another; all produced emotions in the House which were hard to control. On the other hand, there were those who felt that the community was being held to ransom by a single vested interest, encouraged by the Opposition of the day for political reasons. The atmosphere in the House was most unpleasant, and explosions threatened almost every day. The miners' eventual victory did not augur well for the Government's pursuit of an acceptable incomes policy.

In a very different way, and not wholly on party lines, feelings were strong over Britain's proposed entry into the

Common Market. The Conservatives had tried and failed to gain entry in 1963. Labour had tried and failed in 1967. The principle of entry had been endorsed on a free vote in the autumn of 1971 by an unexpectedly large majority, 356 to 244. But when the Bill was introduced and the whips were on, a very different situation arose. The bitter differences within the two major parties made things worse. The majority for the Bill on Second Reading was miniscule. The Committee Stage was taken on the floor of the House, and my unfortunate Deputies and their colleagues from the Chairmen's Panel had a very hard time of it. There were endless points of order, procedural arguments, and an unsuccessful motion criticizing the Chairman of Ways and Means for one of his rulings. Apart from proceedings on the Bill itself, hardly a day passed without an effort to pursue the controversy at Question Time or in some other way.

The Government also undertook a radical reorganization of local government. The control of water resources was refashioned. The organization of the National Health Service was changed. Whatever the rights or wrongs of these decisions, there was much ill-feeling and acrimonious debate.

Northern Ireland remained a running sore. The Government decided to abolish Stormont, and attempted to rule Ulster directly from Westminster. This split the Ulster Unionists. The violence not only escalated in Ulster, but in due course was carried across the Irish Sea to England.

As the confrontation with the unions and the miners' strike had made an acceptable incomes policy almost impossible, the Government had to legislate, in spite of everything that had been said by so many during the election campaign. There was a second confrontation with the miners in mid-winter 1973-4.

The Government had begun with a strong feeling that the 'lame ducks' in industry should not be helped out by the Government. The Industry Act of 1972 gave the impression of a change of direction.

A bitterly contested Housing Finance Bill, always a sore subject, was passed.

Prime Minister's Question Time on Tuesdays and Thursdays each week was marred by personal hostility between Harold Wilson and Edward Heath.

In addition, the Government suffered a grievous blow from the death of Iain Macleod, the new Chancellor of the Exchequer, only a few weeks after the election. Later the resignation of Maudling from the Home Office was also a serious loss.

Many heads had already been shaken at the reflationary measures of the first two years or so of the Parliament and the idea of bursting through to growth and success, but finally the decision of the oil-producing countries to increase the price of oil was a damaging blow to any hopes of containing inflation, at all events for some considerable time.

The Government were committed to drastic changes. An overweighted legislative programme was inevitable. It was also necessary for the Government to cope with a multitude of national and international problems, arising from day to day, such as those caused by a floating pound, and the large increases in the cost of imported raw materials.

One felt that a Government with a secure majority and at least two spells of office would have had its work cut out to cope with all this.

As it was, the majority was small, and eroded by some sensational Liberal victories at by-elections. The Parliament ended with bitter feelings between the two main parties. It was an unpleasant task to have to try to restrain them.

The second Parliament lasted from 6th March to 31st July 1974 (adjourned until 15th October but in fact dissolved during the recess).

The February general election had somewhat surprisingly

ended with no Party having a majority in the House of
Commons.

The strengths were

| | |
|---|---|
| Labour | 301 |
| Conservative | 296 |
| Liberal | 14 |
| United Ulster Unionists (U.U.U.) | 11 |
| Scottish National Party (S.N.P.) | 7 |
| Plaid Cymru (the Welsh Nationalists) | 2 |
| Fitt (S.D.L.P. Ulster) | 1 |
| Taverne (Lincoln, Social Democrat) | 1 |
| Milne (Blyth, Independent Labour) | 1 |
| Mr Speaker | 1 |

The Conservatives had done much worse than they
had expected to earlier in the year. The Liberals had
failed to make a breakthrough. The U.U.U. had swept
the board in Northern Ireland, except against Fitt in
Belfast, West. The S.N.P. were well pleased, as were the
two Plaid Cymru newcomers.

The most significant factor, however, was that the
Conservatives could no longer rely upon the solid support
of Northern Ireland Members. Until just before the 1970–
1974 Parliament this had varied in number, during my
time in the House from 12 to 10 votes. Bernadette Devlin
had won Mid-Ulster from the Unionists at a by-election
in 1969 and held it at the general election. McManus
had won Fermanagh and Tyrone as a Unity candidate,
Paisley had won North Antrim as an Independent Unionist,
and Fitt had held Belfast. Even so, there remained eight
on the whole consistent supporters of the Conservative
Government. In March 1974, this support had completely
disappeared. There were eleven U.U.U. Members, not
committed in any way to supporting the Conservatives,
and Fitt, who usually voted with the Labour Party.

My re-election as Speaker took place in the way already

described (pages 145–6), but before it happened what might have proved a troublesome matter presented itself. The two Plaid Cymru Members demanded the right to take the oath of allegiance in Welsh. Every Member has to take this oath, the Speaker first, before he or she can function as a Member in the House. Gwynfor Evans, the Plaid Cymru leader, had been returned at a by-election for Carmarthen in July 1966. After taking the oath in English, he had asked permission to take it in Welsh. This was refused by Speaker King, and although it had been suggested that the Committee on Procedure should look at the matter for the future, this had not been done.

As the son of a Welsh-speaking father, I was not un-sympathetic. After consulting my advisers, I said that provided Members took the oath in English, which is the language of Parliament, they could also take it in Welsh. Any Member could take it in any language provided that Member also took it in English.

I thought that the two Members concerned were slightly disappointed that I had deprived them of the chance of a public protest on behalf of the Welsh language. They riposted with the claim that they must be allowed to take the oath in Welsh first. I said that I did not care in what order they took it or in how many different languages, but before they were presented to me in the Chair by the Clerk, they must have taken the oath in English. That was that, and several Welsh Members of the Labour, Conservative and Liberal Parties also took it in Welsh.

In the speeches during my re-election as Speaker, some Members referred to the Speaker's task of protecting minorities, adding that in that House even the Government party was a minority.

I tried at once to gain the confidence of the new minorities. I saw the Chairman and two Deputy Chair-men of the U.U.U., Harry West, Paisley and Craig, who controlled that coalition. I saw Donald Stewart, the leader, and Douglas Henderson, the Whip, of the S.N.P., and the two Plaid Cymru Members. I tried to impress upon them that my concern for the rights of minorities was genuine. I would try to protect them and help them in any way I could. I was a friend not an enemy. They could talk about their plans to me in the knowledge that I would respect their confidences, and, within the rules of order, give them fair treatment.

On the whole we got on well together. At times one or more complained that they had not had their chance to ask supplementary questions on a statement or a P.N.Q., but I think that on reflection they realized that I could not call a representative of every minority on every occasion.

In the Queen's Speech the new Government announced their intention to end the State of Emergency, to repeal the Industrial Relations Act, to deal with prices, rents, and the tax system, and to ensure the orderly growth of incomes on a voluntary basis.

The Leader of the House, by custom, winds up the debate on the Queen's Speech for the Government. On this occasion Ted Short had rather a rough ride, and was interrupted more than seemed fair. Pardoe, the Liberal Member for North Cornwall, had an altercation with me about the putting of more than one amendment to a vote at the end of the debate. I had to say, as I have already explained, that the rules of order did not permit me to do so after 10 p.m. on that day. He called me a 'Two Party Speaker'. I did not hear it at the time, but read it next day in the Official Report. I raised it in the House, and Pardoe apologized.

As a result of this incident, the Committee on Procedure reported in favour of a suggestion which I had made to it, whereby more than one vote would be possible after 10 p.m. on occasions like the debate on the Queen's Speech at the opening of a new session.

There was some bad temper shown during Question Time, but I had the feeling of a phoney war.

It was thought that another election so soon would be very unpopular, and the Party considered to be responsible would suffer. The Conservatives therefore felt that they must be careful not to defeat the Government and give them the opportunity to go to the country. The Government would say that they had not been given a fair chance, and that it was all the fault of the Opposition.

The result was that in April, May and June, the attacks by the Opposition were somewhat muted. Nor was the Government itself very provocative.

By the second half of June, it was clear that there could be no election before the autumn, but that it was almost inevitable then. The two sides began to bare their teeth.

On Labour's plans for industry, the Government was defeated twice by 311 to 290 votes on 20th June. On 27th June they were again defeated on rates by 298 to 289, and so it continued.

During this period the troubles of the Chair and indeed of all Members were much increased by industrial troubles in Her Majesty's Stationery Office. This office prints all House of Commons' documents, and the Official Report. During July 1974, we frequently had to rely on Xeroxed copies of the order paper, amendments, and the Official Report. I have already described how this was raised as a matter of privilege, and the ruling which I felt I had to give on that occasion (page 104).

To sum up, this was not a difficult House of Commons to manage, although it did present interesting and novel problems.

My third Parliament as Speaker began on 22nd October 1974. My re-election as Speaker again proceeded smoothly. The Leader of the House came to see me and said that the Government proposed to support my re-election, but he assumed that I would not want to remain as Speaker during the whole length of another Parliament, should it run its full course. I replied that I thought it would be improper for me to enter into any undertakings, but that he could safely make certain assumptions. If the Parliament lasted five years, I would be over seventy-five at the end of it. I certainly would not wish to endure my arduous responsibilities until that age.

When the House met on 22nd October, it was in rather a subdued mood. There were no cheers for the leaders of the two main parties when they came into the Chamber. J. P. W. Mallalieu, younger brother of Lance, the second Deputy Chairman of Ways and Means from November 1972 until the end of that Parliament, proposed my re-election. Derek Walker-Smith again seconded the proposal. Both were old friends, first elected in 1945 at the same time as I had been. They made charming speeches, and Derek told a story which I had not heard before. He referred to a nineteenth-century Speaker whose procession was witnessed one day by an American visitor to the House. The American looked entranced at the spectacle of the procession, and in particular at the Head Door-keeper leading it with stately tread and majestic mien. His host invited his comments. 'Why, great,' he said, 'just great. Your Speaker is sure a swell guy. But say— who is that ugly bastard in the wig, following behind?'

Strauss was again in the Chair. After the proposer and seconder had spoken, he rose to put the Question before I had had a chance to speak. I had to rise and interrupt him, which is why the record of my speech begins with the words 'Mr Strauss, I am very glad to have caught your eye', a formula which I suspect had not been used by any of my predecessors. There were no further speeches, and the formalities passed off smoothly. In particular George Strauss's speech of congratulation moved me very much indeed.

The new House was quite different from its predecessors. The Labour Party had not won its decisive victory. The Liberals were bitterly disappointed. Their appeal, 'a

plague upon both your Labour and Conservative houses',
had failed, and they had actually lost a seat or two. The
U.U.U. coalition had sustained a single casualty. Their
leader, Harry West, lost in Fermanagh and Tyrone, but
they had added to their strength Enoch Powell in place
of Captain Orr. The S.N.P. were delighted with their
increased poll, and their four successes over Conservatives,
making them eleven strong. They had won Galloway
by 30 votes and East Dunbartonshire by 22 votes; a Conservative majority of about 9,000 in Perth and East
Perthshire had been wiped out, and in South Angus a
Conservative majority of over 5,000 had been turned
into an S.N.P. one of 1,800. They had come within 53
votes of winning Kinross and West Perthshire, Alec
Douglas-Home's old seat. On the other hand, Mrs Ewing's
majority in Moray and Nairn had been cut to 367. Gwynfor
Evans had gained Carmarthen comfortably to make the
third Plaid Cymru Member. The two Labour Independents
had fallen by the wayside, Taverne at Lincoln and Milne
at Blyth. As for the two big Parties, Labour had increased
from 301 Members to 319, and the Conservatives had
fallen from 296 to 276.

The Conservatives were immersed in a leadership
problem. It was not resolved until Margaret Thatcher
succeeded Heath three months later. Their front bench
was then radically changed, and it took some time for the
Party to settle down.

On the Government side, the Labour Party had apparently moved to the left. The activities of the Tribune
Group led to the setting up by the moderates of what
was called the Manifesto Group. Rudenesses between
Government and Opposition were certainly equalled by
those exchanged on the Labour back benches. When I
left the Chair, the outcome of this particular confrontation
was still not clear.

The first nine months of the Parliament were dominated
by the Common Market Referendum. Originally bitterly

opposed by the pro-Marketeers, it was increasingly accepted as inevitable. The result was a triumph for those in favour, even Scotland and Ulster voting for remaining in the E.E.C. I must pause to spare a word of praise for those pro-Market Labour Members, particularly in Scotland and Wales, who had the courage to campaign against Labour Party and T.U.C. Conference decisions, to the fury of many of their colleagues. Equally I must praise that minority of anti-Market Conservatives who fought on against overwhelming odds.

As soon as the Referendum campaign was over, inflation resumed its place as the dominant issue. It was then accompanied by steadily rising unemployment figures. There was also fierce argument about the extent and incidence cuts in Government expenditure. When I relinquished my office, these matters were dominating the House and causing bitter dissension within the Labour Party.

Deep divergences of opinion were also becoming apparent about devolution. Almost daily there were shouts of 'Scottish oil'. 'North Sea Oil', 'Shetland Oil'. The S.N.P. Members were very vocal and confident.

Quite frequently there were uncomplimentary noises from the Government side about the House of Lords. Its value as a revising Chamber, to tidy up legislation hurried through the Commons, was obvious. It was also accepted that in the end the Lords would always defer to the will of the elected House. But it was a useful whipping boy, and I was amused to hear some quite surprising Members issuing clarion calls intended to warm the cockles of left-wing hearts.

My conclusions after eighteen months of this, my third House of Commons as Speaker, were that the feelings between the two sides of the House were not as bitter as in my first House as Speaker. But this House was less easy to control than the second. The divisions within the Labour Party were deep; although Margaret Thatcher herself had begun well, the Conservative Party had not yet found itself after the change in leadership and reconstitution of the Front Bench; the Liberals were disappointed; the Ulster Unionists were wary and rather uncertain; the S.N.P. Members were in danger of being over-confident. This is very much an interim impression; much can and no doubt will change.

# VIII

# Whither Parliament?

As I looked down from the Chair for the last time at the House, I had mixed feelings—nostalgic memories of the past thirty years, gratification at the agreeable speeches being made, and thoughts for the future.

I was prejudiced. From the age of sixteen my ambition had been to become a Member of Parliament. I was first adopted as a prospective candidate in April 1927, over forty-nine years before. I fought the 1929 election when I was twenty-four. I had been a Member for over thirty years. Apart from politics, I had built up a considerable practice at the Bar on the Northern Circuit. During the last war, I had occupied positions of some responsibility in the Army. I had from time to time been associated with a variety of public companies. But my true love remained the House of Commons.

I admit at once that I had had more than my share of good fortune. Elected in 1945, in an election disastrous for the Conservatives, I had got to know the House as an Opposition Member, in itself no bad thing, but also as a Member of an Opposition very limited in numbers. As a back-bencher, I became secretary of the Conservative committee on financial affairs. I served under three chairmen—Oliver Stanley, Oliver Lyttelton and Rab Butler, three very different but remarkable personalities.

Oliver Stanley was a brilliant House of Commons speaker,

a master of the rapier not the bludgeon. I remember in very early days sitting beside an old Labour Member, while Stanley was speaking. 'This', he said, 'is the fellow I like to hear. He's the best of the lot.' His premature death was a tragedy.

As a Minister, I served under four Prime Ministers — Churchill, Eden, Macmillan and Douglas-Home. I have distinctive memories of them: Churchill's courtesy and carefulness in discussing at length Foreign Office matters with one who was only a junior Minister; Eden's brilliant diplomatic gifts, his intuition, charm and ability to command affectionate loyalty; Macmillan's wit and erudition, his power of analysis of people and events, his conversation; Alec Douglas-Home's simplicity of approach and shrewd common-sense judgments.

The 'shadows' who opposed me from time to time were Nye Bevan, Alf Robens, Harold Wilson and Jim Callaghan, with all of whom personally I was on friendly terms, whatever they said or thought about my capabilities. My pair was for some years 'Manny' Shinwell, in earlier days I believe an abrasive character but in my time a very lovable one.

For me the Commons had meant much more than front-bench confrontations. When I was on the back benches, I was a member of the Estimates Committee, the Committee of Privileges, the Procedure Committee and the Services Committee. For some these would have seemed just one dreary chore after another, but I thoroughly enjoyed them all.

Then there had been the theatre of the House itself. Politicians are not popular as a species; they have rude things said about them all the time. In the Commons, however, they are a fascinating study, man by man, woman by woman. Triumph one day, failure the next, a mistake here, a tactical success there, drama, bathos, the whole gamut of human experience. The House is an excellent judge of character. Conceit, deviousness, the shoddy and the second-rate, the bully, the toad-eater, simplicity, sincerity and genuine compassion, all are discerned sooner or later.

Of course it may be said, 'This is all sentiment and sentimentality. The place is impotent, inefficient, out of date, not properly equipped and unrepresentative.' That is not at all the way in which I had looked at it, nor do I think of it like that today.

The accusation of impotence is no new one. Kenneth Rose in his book *The Later Cecils* (1975) quotes a letter from the third Marquess of Salisbury (three times Prime Minister) written to his eldest son in 1881. The son had been asked to speak in Liverpool. His father wrote advising acceptance of the invitation on the ground that 'Power is more and more leaving Parliament and going to the platform.' The same sort of thing has been said many times since, although the residuary legatee changes. It is the trade unions, the City, the Press, public boards, the gnomes of Zurich, the multi-national companies or the super powers.

The truth is that we no longer rule a great colonial empire; we can no longer be self-sufficient in defence; we cannot manage our affairs in splendid isolation. External economic influences largely determine our policies. The E.E.C., NATO, GATT, OPEC, O.E.C.D., and multi-national interests and concerns reduce to a minimum the possibility of our taking independent national action which affects other countries. At home the T.U.C. and the C.B.I. demand their say, and the scale of operations of the nationalized industries and services limit the Government's freedom of action, and often compel it to do what it really does not want to do.

The House of Commons can influence day-to-day decisions, but for many years the Government, not the House, has possessed the executive power. If a Government cannot command a majority in the House, it will fall. Neville Chamberlain's resignation in 1940 was due to a vote in the

6

House (incidentally on a motion to adjourn), but that was wartime. It is not so much the influence of Parliament that has declined. It is the Government's power of independent action.

None the less there are still many aspects of the work of the House which require thought. I will try to dispose of some of the less important ones first.

New Members complain at once about the conditions under which they have to work. I sympathize with them to some extent. They come from well-appointed offices, academic environments or jobs in industry where the facilities match the requirements, or where there is little paper work. They are elected to the House and suddenly find themselves oppressed by a cascade of letters, Official Reports, White Papers, Green Papers, Blue Books, and memoranda on every conceivable topic. They have a locker, a desk, and a secretary with a filing cabinet some distance away. Members of the Bar, accustomed to the discomforts of what was the average County Court or Magistrates' Court, are more tolerant. But I accept that attempts at improvement must be pushed forward at reasonable cost and within the limits imposed by a Palace of Westminster not purpose-built, at all events for a 1976 Parliament.

As Leader of the House in 1963–4, I was made aware at once of the hardships caused by the underpayment of Members. I pressed for the setting up of the Lawrence Committee and managed to extract a commitment from the Parties that they would accept any reasonable proposals, no matter who won the 1964 election. I was particularly anxious about some appropriate pension provision. I firmly believe that Members should be reimbursed for expenses properly incurred and should be paid enough to be able, without hardship, to avoid yielding to direct or indirect financial inducements. The changes made in July 1975 seemed to me then to be about right, although in view of the considerable increase in the scale of allowances, perhaps there should be a closer scrutiny of their use.

Another hardy annual is the argument about the hours of sitting. Why cannot the House sit normal office hours, say 10 a.m. to 6 p.m.? That would mean prayers at 10, Questions from 10.05 to 11, P.N.Q.s and statements at 11, then the business of the day, with the House sitting on through lunch, and, unless the rule were suspended, the half-hour adjournment from 5.30 to 6 p.m. Applications for P.N.Q.s or debates under Standing Order No. 9 must now reach the Speaker at noon, i.e., three and a half hours before 3.30 p.m. when they are taken. That would mean by 7.30 a.m. if they came on at 11 a.m., and would make it impossible for the Speaker to receive the necessary advice. Therefore notice would have to be given by say 5.30 p.m. on the day before. As to the House rising at 6 p.m., it now seldom rises at 10.30 p.m., even with the known dislike of late hours and their general inconvenience. I believe that the rule would be in danger of suspension almost every day for several hours, at a time when the incentives to brevity would be much weaker. Morning sittings would not have achieved their purpose.

Apart from that, I believe that they would make life very much more difficult for a great many Members.

Ministers, except when they have a Bill in Standing Committee, are free in the mornings to deal with their Departments. There are Cabinet and Cabinet Committee meetings. Appointments and luncheon engagements can be made with some certainty. With regular morning sittings, I do not believe that Ministers could exercise proper control of their Departments. With Ministers pinned down in the Commons, more and more power would pass to officials.

Private Members can, under the present system, attend to their businesses or practise their professions. Employment in the law, the City, the media, and business generally is just possible if attendance in the House is not obligatory until say 5 p.m. The House is a much better balanced place if some Members derive knowledge of what is going on in the outside world other than from constituents or newspapers or radio and television. It may be an old-fashioned view, but I strongly believe that a House consisting of Members forbidden to engage in anything except politics would be a ghastly place.

It is argued that the present system could not work without about half the Members being prepared to be full-timers. Certain committees have to meet in the morning, and have to be manned. While these Members work hard, others can add perhaps substantially to their Parliamentary salaries by attending board meetings or practising in the Courts. This is said to be unfair. I think that there is sub-stance in this complaint, and I would favour an experi-mental period in which those who served on committees in the mornings received some extra remuneration in the form of an attendance allowance.

I have always been in favour of an experiment in the broadcasting and televising of the proceedings in Parlia-ment. I spoke in favour when the proposal was defeated by one vote in November 1966. I had to accept the view of a majority in 1974 that the experiment should be limited to radio broadcasting. That experiment produced some useful guide lines for the future. With regard to television, we had been assured about ten years ago that a new camera would be ready by about 1970 which could televise the House with only marginal increases in the lighting required. I do not think that it has yet been produced.

There is also the problem of editing. It is argued that proceedings in Parliament cannot have a channel to themselves. I doubt it, but that is a long technical story. In fact it would be too much of a good thing or of what-ever description is appropriate to the House's endeavours. Therefore the issue is how best to use say at most an hour a day, including any item appearing in a news programme. The editing during the experiment in sound broadcasting was, in my view, excellent. On television it would be more difficult, but I do not believe impossible.

There are obvious problems, for example Question Time. Each Member has an Order Paper on which the questions are printed. When a question is called, it is not read out. The Speaker says 'Mr ——'. Mr ·—— gets up and says 'Number —, Sir'. That is all. It makes it impossible for the listener or viewer to follow what is happening. However, in spite of all these difficulties, I think that the public should hear and see more of what goes on in the House. I hope that the problems, which are considerable, will be solved. No doubt the reporting of Parliamentary debates was opposed two hundred years ago for much the same reasons as are advanced today against broadcasting the proceedings.

There is a constant stream of complaint about the procedures and customs of the House. As the rules have evolved over a period of seven centuries, this is not surprising. On one occasion, a Member protested vigorously that it was a waste of time for the Speaker to read out to the House the Queen's Speech already made by her in the House of Lords. The reason for its being read again was the determination of the Commons to assert its independence of the Lords. It was not prepared to accept something read out there; the Speech had to be read out also in the Commons. There are other similar customs, for which at one time or another there was good reason. Their continuance did not worry me, although I suppose a case of a sort could be made out for their abandonment.

Outside critics do not realize the extent to which changes and improvements in procedure are constantly being made. The House does not complacently accept that all is perfect, and that any change would be for the worse. What has happened in the last ten years proves this. Debates in the whole House on a Bill can be restricted. It is now technically possible by means of a Second Reading Committee, Standing Committee, Report Committee and

no debate on Third Reading, for a non-controversial
Bill to pass all its stages without debate on the floor of the
House. Extra time has been found for Private Members'
Bills. Part of the Committee Stage of the Finance Bill is
now taken in Standing Committee. Statutory Instruments
are considered on their merits by a Standing Committee.
The Scottish and Welsh Grand Committees, and the
Standing Committee on Regional Affairs can have their
own debates. Specialist Committees have been set up.
There is an Expenditure Committee, to scrutinize public
expenditure, with wide terms of reference and powers.
In quite different fields, the 'count' (requiring forty members to be present in the Chamber within four minutes
of the calling of the count) has been abolished, Standing
Order No. 9 about emergency debates has been redrafted.
Members' interests have to be registered. And so it goes
on, with constant attempts at improvement. I certainly
have not agreed with all of them, but the idea of a House
obstinately refusing to change its rules and customs is
quite false.

On day-to-day matters, in my opinion, as I later indicate,
Question Time should be extended and the form of questions which can be put to the Prime Minister should be
reviewed. The Chair should have a discretion to enforce
a limit on the length of speeches, in certain limited circumstances. Means of checking abuses of Standing Order
No. 9 could easily be devised. I would like to see changes
in the procedure under which the Speaker chairs conferences on electoral reform. If the Government with the
agreement of the Opposition indicate their wish that the
Speaker should preside over a conference to consider
certain electoral matters, the Speaker should then act as
follows. He should choose three or four experienced Members
to examine with him the particular topics designated,
and to decide what papers upon them would be required
by way of evidence, and what witnesses should be asked
to prepare oral evidence. When that has been done, and

the papers received, a conference with a larger membership, but not exceeding twenty, should be convened, and
the material already assembled put before it. Of course
other papers could be called for and other witnesses summoned as proved necessary. I believe that this method
would save a lot of time, both for the Speaker and for the
members of the conference.

On the preparation of legislation, I consider that the
Renton Committee made an excellent report. I hope it
will be followed up vigorously.

Having tried to deal with all these matters, some important, others not so, I come to five basic questions
affecting the future of the House of Commons. They are as
follows.

(1)   What is the task of Parliament to-day?
(2)   What is its role within the E.E.C.?
(3)   How will it be affected by the various plans for
      devolution?
(4)   Does the electoral system require reform?
(5)   What type of M.P. do we now need?

## (1) What Should be the Tasks of Parliament in Present Circumstances?

Parliament has to function as a legislature. Throughout
most of my time, the load has been excessive, and the
quality of the product inferior. The rush to pass new laws,
the almost pathetic belief that the millennium can be
achieved by Act of Parliament, has produced certain results.
Most of us are unable to make out our own tax returns.
Employers and employees do not know their statutory
obligations and rights. The same applies to landlords
and tenants. Each year, legislative confusion appears to
become worse confounded. John Peyton put it well when
he referred to the Renton Report as a 'restrained and
politely worded reminder of that legislative misconduct

of which all Governments have been guilty as initiators, and to which all of us have been accessories'. When I left the Chair there were ugly rumours current concerning the possibility of fixed timetables for all Bills, in order to make it easier to get them through the House of Commons.

Secondly Parliament must be the forum where important issues can be debated. Owing to the overloaded legislative programme, such debates are not frequent. Nor do I think that either Party when in Opposition has made the best use of its right to choose topics for debate on Supply Days. Debates on foreign affairs, defence, law and order, unemployment, investment in industry, agriculture and regional policies do not take place often enough. Too frequently some subject of short-term party political interest is chosen.

Thirdly the task of Parliament, particularly of the House of Commons, is to scrutinize the behaviour of the Executive, Ministers and their officials, the nationalized industries and public corporations. In spite of all the criticism, I believe that this is done by the House on the whole as well and as expeditiously as by any other comparable assembly. But there are flaws and gaps in our methods, and some of them would not be very difficult to put right. Having had some leisure to think about what is practicable, I come down in favour of the following steps.

I would extend Question Time, starting prayers at 2.25 p.m. on an ordinary day, beginning questions at 2.30 and continuing to 3.45. On Fridays I would have prayers at 10.25 a.m., questions from 10.30 to 11.30, and the House rising at 5 p.m. I would change the rules with regard to Prime Minister's questions, and no longer allow the 'pegs' (Will he visit such and such a place? What are his engagements for today? When will he next attend the meeting of a particular body?). In return, the Prime Minister would have to exercise more sparingly his right to transfer questions to other Ministers. One day a week, he might answer for thirty minutes.

Next, and equally important, I would maintain and extend the system of specialist committees, for example the work of the sub-committees of the Expenditure Committee. But I would make it mandatory that the Government's reactions to the reports of these bodies be published within a fixed period of say four to six weeks, and that the reports and departmental answers be debated within eight weeks thereafter. There can be nothing more frustrating than to spend months investigating a particular matter, reporting on it, usually across Party lines, and then having to wait a long time for the Department's replies. The final indignity comes when time cannot be found for a debate on the floor of the House.

If the work of these committees does receive proper consideration, I think there would be a case for the House itself not sitting after say 4 p.m. one day a week, so that the committees could get on with their work uninterrupted. But this idea is subject to the mandatory caveats which I have just mentioned.

There was, during my last year or two, a lot of talk about a research assistant for every Member, and some financial provision was made. I think that the need is there, but I doubt the proposed remedy. I would prefer to see the resources of the House of Commons Library still further expanded, and each Select Committee or sub-committee enabled to have for each particular inquiry more advisers technically qualified in the required field.

Under this heading, I return to an old hobby-horse. I believe that the Leader of the House should have no other government responsibilities. He should be left free to supervise, perhaps with an unofficial committee of two or three others, all these extremely important House of Commons' matters.

## (2) What is the Role of the House of Commons, now that the United Kingdom is in the E.E.C.?

I give a guarded answer to this question. I believe that, in the Council of Ministers, the right of veto should continue for a time which I certainly would not be prepared to specify. Similarly, while the mechanics of scrutiny by the House of Common Market legislation needs constant examination, and while safeguards are no doubt required against obstruction or filibustering, I believe that for some time the House would be right to insist on an independent voice. Abuse of that right would be counter-productive, and, in my view, the staunchest pro-European would be wise to concede it. Similarly, those who seek to hurry on direct elections to the European Parliament should be clear in their minds as to the effect upon Westminster.

## (3) How will the House of Commons be Affected by the Various Plans for Devolution?

This is dangerous ground on which to tread. I served for over two years on the Royal Commission on the Constitution. If one could start again from scratch, I would be in favour of a large measure of Home Rule for the English regions as well as for Scotland, Wales and Northern Ireland. In the north west, we are over six million strong, larger than any of those three. Over-centralization, whether the Whitehall Department is in London, Cardiff, Bootle or Glasgow, is just as irritating for us as for anybody. Unfortunately we cannot start from scratch. Whatever happens, another layer of officialdom, or elected representatives, must not be introduced. This will be a matter of general concern throughout the rest of this Parliament, and I had better not comment further, except for one apparently trite but usually forgotten truism. If obligations are imposed on new bodies, others must be relieved of them.

## (4) Does the Electoral System Require Reform?

The present system is obviously imperfect. I doubt whether the voting practices were perfect even in the city states of Greece. The defect most easy to remedy is the large difference in the number of voters, comparing one constituency with another. In October 1974 there were 310,271 voters in the four constituencies of Bebington and Ellesmere Port, Birkenhead, Wallasey and Wirral, returning four Members. There were 398,940 voters in the Liverpool constituencies of Edgehill, Garston, Kirkdale, Scotland and Exchange, Toxteth, Walton, Wavertree and West Derby, returning eight Members. The four divisions of Newcastle-upon-Tyne with 187,991 voters returned the same number of Members as the 310,271 voters in the Wirral peninsula. Newcastle Central with 25,156 voters had equal representation in the House as Wirral with 93,135. This is a nonsense. I would hope that the guide lines for the Boundary Commission can be speedily re-examined.

It is also unfair, but not so easy to remedy, that the same Party could be second in every seat in an area, or even third, and, in spite of the substantial number of votes cast for its candidates, have no representation. This has been the Liberal complaint for a long time. It could also be the complaint of the Labour Party in the south east or south west, and of the Conservative Party in almost all the big cities. The difficulty is to know what to do about it. I hope that by now a Speaker's conference on electoral reform has been set up to examine the various kinds of proportional representation or other systems now being advocated. I have no fixed ideas. The argument against the alternative vote, in other words that in a three-cornered contest the voters should indicate their second preferences, always used to be that it would lead to unsavoury bargains between the various Party machines. I doubt whether nowadays voters are so docile as to allow their votes to be 'delivered' in this way. If there is to be a change, the

system under which University Members were elected
when I first entered the House bears consideration. It
was described as proportional representation (single trans-
ferable vote).

## (5) *What Type of Members of Parliament do we now need?*

I hope it is clear that I am not complacent about the
House of Commons, its procedures and other constitutional
arrangements. Constant review and reform are necessary,
and I have tried to make some suggestions.

It is not, however, the perfection of procedures or the
excellence of facilities that really matter. It is the men
and women who use them. Some Members aspire to
becoming a kind of pocket encyclopaedia of knowledge
and statistical data. They would like to be regarded as
'well informed'. They feel their mission is to advise or
direct Ministers from their own superior knowledge. Lord
Salisbury's words in 1877 about experts applies very much
to the parliamentary expert. He wrote to Lord Lytton
' ... you should never trust experts ... they are required to
have their strong wine diluted by a very large admixture
of insipid commonsense. Many times have I seen the need
for this.'

The view which I share is that apart from this constant
scrutiny of the executive, a Member of Parliament has
two roles to fulfil. He or she can mitigate hardship, prevent
injustice, help individuals and act as a speedy means
of communication between the ordinary citizen and the
ministerial mandarins. Secondly, when some great issue
presents itself, the House of Commons must function as
the common jury of the nation. It is a remarkable illustra-
tion of this that the free vote on the Common Market
in October 1971 was not very different from that of the
country as a whole in the Referendum nearly four years
later. What is needed to sustain both these roles is character,
common sense and judgment. People possessing those

qualities are those whom constituency selection committees should be seeking. In spite of the occasional black sheep, and those who do not quite meet the requirements, these qualities have been the hallmarks of Westminster. So let aspirants to membership of the House be not cast down. They will have to face unrelenting abuse of their species. But they will find their reward in the respect and good wishes of those whose needs as individuals they try to meet, and in the fact that from time to time they do indeed make history.

# Glossary

I have tried to define briefly some of the terms and phrases used in connection with the work of the House. In many cases the definitions are incomplete because of the need for brevity. Again I acknowledge my debt to Erskine May.

*Act*: a law which has been passed by both Houses of Parliament and received the Royal Assent.

*Adjournment motion*: one to interrupt a debate, or to terminate a sitting of the House; the motion to adjourn is often the peg on which to hang a general debate; at the end of each sitting day, a half hour's debate is initiated by a Private Member.

*Affirmative procedure*: *see* Statutory Instruments.

*Back-benchers*: *see* Front-benchers.

*Bar of the House*: a line marked out on the floor of the House opposite the Speaker's Chair—on the far side of it Members are technically not in the House and cannot intervene in the proceedings.

*Bill*: a proposed law which has not yet passed through the stages necessary to make it an Act. *See also* Stages of a Bill.

*By-election*: an election between general elections in a single constituency to fill a vacancy.

*Chair*: a convenient way of referring to the Speaker, his Deputies and their relationship to the House.

*Chairman of Ways and Means*: Deputy Speaker. *See also* Ways and Means.

*Chairmen's Panel*: not less than ten Members appointed by the Speaker, each session, to act as Chairmen of Standing Committees: they can also act if necessary as Chairmen of Committees of the whole House.

*Chiltern Hundreds*: a notional office of profit under the Crown disqualifying a Member from continuing as such; acceptance of it is a way Members resign in the course of a Parliament.

*Clerk*: the chief officer of the House, dealing with business and procedural matters. He is also Accounting Officer.

*Clerks Assistant*: the Clerk's two senior assistants.

*Closure*: a motion to end a debate: it can only be moved with the permission of the Chair.

*Collect the voices*: *see* Question.

*Committee*: *see* Select Committee, Standing Committee.

*Commons*: the elected House of Parliament (with 635 Members after the general election of October 1974).

*Consolidated Fund Bill*: the Bill authorizing ordinary annual expenditure.

*Delegated legislation*: *see* Statutory Instruments.

*Deliverer of the Vote*: the officer of the House who supervises the provision of official papers for Members through the Vote Office.

*Dissolution*: the ending of a Parliament by proclamation.

*Division*: the Members dividing into the aye and noe lobbies, to vote. *See also* Question.

*Division bell*: bells which ring throughout the precincts and in some places outside the Palace of Westminster to make it known that a Division is taking place.

*Division lobbies*: the narrow rooms as long as the House itself through which Members pass to vote—the aye lobby to the right of the Speaker's Chair, the noe lobby to the left of it.

*Doorkeepers*: officials of the House who prevent persons who are not entitled to from entering the chamber or its precincts and, among other duties, lock the doors of the division lobbies. *See also* Question.

*Emergency debate*: *see* Standing Order No. 9.

*Estimates*: particulars of public expenditure which the House has to approve.

*Father of the House*: the Member with the longest period of continuous service in the House.

*Front-benchers*: those Members who sit on the front benches on the sides of the gangways, nearer to the Speaker's Chair: the Government side on his right, the Opposition leaders on his left. All others are called back-benchers.

*Gangway*: the passages about half-way down the House on either side to enable Members to reach their places.

*Guillotine*: *see* Timetable motion.

*Hansard*: the verbatim daily Official Report of the proceedings of the House, so called because Messrs Hansards were the House's printers. Now it is printed by the Stationery Office. Answers to written questions are included.

*Hybrid Bills*: Bills which are public Bills but may affect private rights. *See also* Private Bills and Public Bills.

*Journal*: the permanent official record of the proceedings of the House.

*Leader of the House*: the Member of the Cabinet in charge of the business of the House. He answers all questions about business.

*Lobby*: the attendance at the House of a number of people interested in some current matter, asking to see their Members of Parliament about it. *See also* Division lobbies, Main lobby, Members' lobby.

*'Lock the doors'*: *see* Question.

*Lords*: the upper, non-elected House of Parliament.

*Lords' Amendment*: amendment passed by the House of Lords affecting a Bill which has completed its stages up to Third Reading in the Commons.

*Mace*: the symbol of the authority of the Speaker, placed upon the Table when the Speaker or his Deputies are in the Chair. When the House is in committee, it is placed underneath the top of the Table.

*Main lobby*: the main or central lobby is in the centre of the Palace. Anyone seeking to see a Member is admitted to it.

*Members' lobby*: the area just outside the Chamber, to which Members, ex-Members, and certain representatives of the Press have access.

*Motion*: a substantive motion put before the House for it to decide: technically it is a new item of business. *See also* Orders of the Day.

*Naming*: one of the disciplinary powers of the Chair—a Member is named if the Member disregards the authority of the Chair; a motion is then moved to suspend that Member from the service of the House.

*Negative procedure*: *see* Statutory Instruments.

*Nineteen-Twenty-Two Committee*: the 1922 Committee is the party committee of Conservative Members usually meeting once a week.

*Nodding through*: if a Member is physically incapacitated in some way, his or her name can be given by a Whip to the tellers in the division and that vote counted, provided the Member is on the premises.

*Northstead*: Steward and Bailiff of the Manor of Northstead is another notional office of profit under the Crown. *See also* Chiltern Hundreds.

*Oath*: the oath of allegiance which must be taken before any Member can function as a Member: a Member is entitled to make affirmation in lieu of taking the oath.

*Order*: calling the House to order, enforcing the Standing Orders.

*Order Paper*: gives the agenda for the day's sitting.

*Orders of the Day*: business already partly considered comes under this heading. *See also* Motion.

*Pairing*: two Members who propose to vote differently on a specific question or series of questions can agree that neither should vote; they pair off with one another. The pair should be registered with their respective Whips' offices.

*Parliamentary Private Secretary*: called P.P.S.; a Member who assists a Minister with his duties in the House, sitting behind him when he is speaking or answering questions, arranging a pair, keeping him in touch with opinions on both sides of the House, etc.; a P.P.S. draws no extra remuneration.

*Patronage Secretary*: the Government Chief Whip.

*P.L.P.*: the Parliamentary Labour Party. All Labour Members belong to it. It usually meets once a week.

*Point of order*: a Member seeking to call the attention of the Chair to a supposed breach of order.

*Positive procedure*: *see* Statutory Instruments.

*Private Bills*: Bills containing provisions for the particular interest or benefit of any person or persons, public company, corporation or local authority.

*Private Members*: those not in the Government.

*Private Members' Bills*: those sponsored by Private Members, not by the Government.

*Private Members' Time*: time allotted to Private Members for Bills or motions.

*Private Notice Question* (*P.N.Q.*): one allowed to be put at short notice if in the Speaker's opinion it is of an urgent character, and relates either to a matter of public importance or to the House's business.

*Privilege*: the rights of the House as a whole and of individual Members, the exercise of which enables them to discharge their functions.

*Privy Councillor*: Member of the Privy Council, and called Right Honourable.

*Prorogation*: the termination of a session of Parliament.

*Public Bills*: Bills dealing with matters of public general interest.

*Question*: at the beginning of a debate, the occupant of the Chair 'proposes' the Question before the House, for example, 'That the Bill be now read a second time'.

The debate follows.

At the end of the debate he 'puts' the question in the same terms.

He then 'collects the voices' by saying, 'As many as are of that opinion say aye: of the contrary noe.'

If there are shouts of aye and noe, he says (perhaps according to the volume of the shouts), 'I think the ayes have it.'

If the shouts continue, he calls 'Clear the lobby.' After two minutes he puts the question again.

If there are still shouts of aye and noe, he says, 'Ayes to the right, noes to the left. Tellers for the ayes Mr X and Mr Y, tellers for the noes, Mr A and Mr B.'

After not less than four more minutes, he calls 'Lock the doors.'

The doors of the division lobbies are locked, so that no more Members can enter them.

The tellers in due course come and stand in a row facing the Speaker beyond the Table. One announces the figures. The Speaker repeats the figures, and announces the decision, for example, 'The ayes have it.'

*Questions*: these are tabled by Members for oral or written answer by a Minister.

*Question time*: the time on Mondays, Tuesdays, Wednesdays and Thursdays each week, between the end of prayers (with a qualification about Private Business) and 3.30 p.m.; Ministers answer according to a roster.

*Reading, First, Second and Third*: *see* Stages of a Bill.

*Recess*: strictly the period between the prorogation of Parliament and its re-assembly for a new session; but generally used for any period longer than a week-end during which the House is adjourned in the course of a session.

*Report Stage*: *see* Stages of a Bill.

*Ruling*: a decision by the Chair on a point of order or a matter of procedure.

*Select Committee*: a number of Members specially named to examine a particular matter or area of inquiry, for example nationalized industries, or Statutory Instruments or House of Commons services.

*Serjeant at Arms*: an officer of the House, appointed by the Queen, with multifarious duties throughout the Commons' part of the Palace of Westminster, such as security, admission of visitors, order in the precincts, accommodation for Members, the Press Gallery, ceremonial attendance upon the Speaker, and so on.

*Shadow Cabinet*: the leader of the official Opposition and his principal colleagues, to each of whom is usually assigned a particular sphere of opposition.

*Stages of a Bill*: The First Reading of a Bill is a formality.

The Second Reading debate is a general one on the merits of the Bill.

The Bill then goes either to a Standing Committee or a committee of the whole House for detailed examination.

After the Committee Stage, there is a Report Stage on the floor of the House, when further detailed examination, but of much shorter duration, takes place.

Then there is the Third Reading, with or without a debate.

The Bill then goes to the Lords, for similar treatment.

If the Lords amend it, those amendments are considered by the whole House of Commons.

*Standing Committee*: between sixteen and fifty Members chosen to represent proportionately the Party strengths in the House. *See also* Stages of a Bill.

*Standing Orders*: the rules regulating the conduct of business by the House.

*Standing Order No. 9*: deals with applications for an emergency debate on a specific and important matter which should have urgent consideration.

*Statutory Instruments*: an Act can give a Minister power to make orders under it; that is delegated legislation: the orders are called Statutory Instruments. The affirmative or positive procedure means that the order does not remain in force beyond a certain period unless Parliament agrees. The negative procedure means that it remains in force unless and until Parliament otherwise orders.

*Strangers*: those who are not Members. 'Strangers' are admitted to various parts of the House, according to certain rules.

*Sub judice matter*: matter awaiting a judicial decision.

*Supply*: the provision of money for public expenditure; on a certain number of what are called 'Supply Days' the Opposition choose the topics for debate.

*Suspension of a Member*: *see* Naming.

*Suspension of the rule*: *see* Ten o'clock rule.

*Table*: the large table in front of the Speaker, on which the Mace is placed; the Clerk and the two Clerk's Assistants sit between the Speaker and the Table.

*Table Office*: deals, under the Clerk, with notices of motions, questions, amendments, the Order Paper, etc. to ensure that Members are in order in what they want to do, and the business of the House is correctly set out.

*Tellers*: the four Members who count the votes of other Members as they pass through the division lobbies. *See also* Question.

*Ten-minute-rule Bill*: one introduced by a Private Member on a subject of that Member's choice, so called because the speech introducing it should not be longer than ten minutes.

*Ten o'clock rule*: from Mondays to Thursdays, the discussion of the business of the day must end at 10 p.m. unless a motion to exempt certain items from the rule has been passed.

*Timetable Motion*: a motion limiting the amount of time to be devoted to a particular stage of a Bill or to several such stages, also called the guillotine.

*Trainbearer*: he attends the Speaker on all ceremonial occasions; he also deals with secretarial work, applications by Members to speak or for adjournment debates, etc.

*Usual channels*: *see* Whips.

*Vote Office*: *see* Deliverer of the Vote.

*Ways and Means*: The Committee of Ways and Means controlled Supply. It was abolished in 1966. Its Chairman became Deputy Speaker in 1853. Since then the Deputy Speaker has also been Chairman of Ways and Means, and the title has survived. The other two Deputies are called the First and Second Deputy Chairman of Ways and Means, respectively.

*Whip*: a summons to attend, stating the business of the House for the week, each item being underlined. A one-line Whip is a request to attend, but indicates there will not be a vote; a two-line Whip means that Members' attendance is essential to vote unless they have registered a firm pair; a three-line Whip is a summons to attend and vote, no pairing being allowed (except by special permission in very exceptional circumstances).

*Whips*: this is the name for the Members who organize the Parties for the business of the House: the two Chief Whips of the two main parties have very heavy responsibilities. They and the Whips of the smaller Parties are what are called 'the usual channels'.

*Who goes home?*: the cry of the Doorkeepers at the rising of the House; no doubt originally so that Members could form groups to go home in greater safety.

*Withdraw*: the Chair can order a Member to withdraw an unparliamentary remark, or to withdraw from the Chamber; if the latter, the Member cannot return during that day's sitting.

*Writ*: there is the general issue of writs for a new Parliament; and also the issue during a Parliament of a writ upon the Speaker's warrant, with the authority of the House if it is sitting, or if not, upon his own authority, for an election to fill a vacancy.

*Written Question*: *see* Questions.

# Index